Social Influence and Genius
– A Leadership Journey

A Better Future for your Business
And the World

Social Influence and Genius
– A Leadership Journey

A Better Future for your Business
And the World

C. Dan McArthur and Vincent Higgins

Tanglewood
Publishing

SOCIAL INFLUENCE AND GENIUS, A LEADERSHIP JOURNEY
Copyright © 2011 C. Dan McArthur and Vincent Higgins

First Edition – October 2011

Published in the United States of America by Tanglewood Publishing

Tanglewood Publishing
3050 Post Oak Blvd, Suite 1750
Houston, TX 77056

ISBN-10: 0-983-6394-1-8
ISBN-13: 978-0-983-63941-1

1. Leadership – Personal Development. 2. Management – Cultural Change.
3. Business – Growth and Profit. 4. Strategy – Wider Impact. I. Title

Design and editing by Christopher Jones

CONTENTS

About the book

Business entropy is one of the biggest challenges for businesses of all sizes. Entropy describes how the purpose, meaning and direction underlying a successful business can lose strength over time.

- Effective Leadership equates to business growth, maximizes profitability and increases survival strength.
- Maligned leadership generates business entropy, costs your organization money and decreases survival strength.

The old way of influencing people by directing them to do things has given way to interacting with them in a way that makes them to want to do things. The changing face of leadership is increasingly concerned with interactivity - drawing people and disparate parts of an organization together in ways that make individuals and organizations whole. Interactivity and its continued focus include and recognize everyone's contribution as a leader to an enterprise's success.

The leadership journey outlined in this book is much more than a self-help guide, it gets to the *heart* of leading organizations. As you continue on your journey with us you will learn a new model of leadership and organizational structure that fits the context to which leadership manifests itself - the events, people and processes within an ever expanding area of influence. You will discover a most vital lesson of success, *Leadership Genius*. Leadership Genius addresses the greatest need of today - the capacity to focus and engage the entire genius of an organization and the community it lives in around vital business objectives while creating and preserving values – utility, social, emotional and spiritual.

The book is a fun read manifested in visual metaphors, brief supporting quotes and action-oriented skill instructions to lead the reader through on-the-job leadership experiences that will demonstrate and reward you with the value that it presents.

-Foreword-

My career in journalism has been punctuated by stories of the failings of leaders.

This issue has been at the center of the downfall of governments and the Asian financial crisis that dominated my years with The Associated Press and Dow Jones. It has also been key, more recently, in my coverage of the collapse of Enron and BP's safety gap for the Financial Times. For this I was named Reporter of the Year in the 2007 British Press Awards.

While these stories underline leadership failure in its extreme, the fact is that most of the news coverage in the world today is negative. There is always some business or another in trouble, whether because it failed to follow best practices, lost touch with its clients or got left behind by technology. The reality is, that to stay off the front page for all the wrong reasons, the world - and business in particular - must focus on "next practices." This is the theme of Social Influence and Genius, which I believe any business - including the energy business I cover - should read to stay relevant in this changing world.

I came across this book through my youngest son, Gabriel, who is a friend of one of the author's children. When Gregory came to play, I met his parents, and a copy of the book was passed along. It is worth noting how often professional relationships begin in such a personal way.

But unless you are the type of leader who is open to listening, learning and new approaches, such an opportunity might be missed. The authors cite a number of case studies throughout the book that illustrate the importance of being open to new opportunities. Perhaps the best of these is about how IBM has consistently reinvented itself to stay relevant.

Instead of suggesting a cookie-cutter approach, McArthur and Higgins encourage corporations to create their own unique plan to build or continue success into the future. "Go beyond current formulas and establish new practices rather than relying on best practices," is a major lesson.

The authors guide readers in how to develop their own formula for success, with a "go deeper'" section on how to put the ideas into practice. This sets it apart from the typical how-to leadership books, which only tell you how to lead by copying what others have done.

What impressed me more than anything in reading this book was the overriding lesson for leaders to build a "leadership culture'" that involves opening lines of communication from the mail room to the boardroom and really listening and learning from people at all levels. This not only generates new ideas and keeps the leadership up-to-date on changes in the marketplace, it also gives workers a sense of really being part of a company and having a stake in its success. What better motivation to do a good job could there be?

Ideas for improvement can come from anywhere, and yet they are so often kept in a cubicle by a disgruntled employee who feels nobody would care what he or she could offer. Creating a business where people at all levels feel valued is key. The authors make a point of noting that leadership exists in everyone. They show how businesses can develop a leadership culture and an organizational structure in which everyone is not only encouraged - but expected - to be a leader.

Of course, this cannot be accomplished overnight. It is a path that a business can only follow when it is ready to let go of what worked yesterday, or the business strategy they first had, and be open to the realities of a changing world. That is the key to ending up an IBM instead of a General Motors, which was once the largest corporation in the US and the largest employer in the world and yet in 2009 found itself filing for bankruptcy protection from creditors.

Sheila McNulty
The Financial Times

-Preface-

Social Influence and Genius
A Leadership Journey

Leadership books fill the shelves of our local bookstores. Some are inches thick and involve years of academic research, others are short inspirational texts filled with platitudes that do not address tangible business issues.

Leadership, simply defined, is a social influence relationship between individuals who depend on each other in a group setting to attain mutual goals. To specifically analyze leadership in business, we are going to need a more detailed definition.

Leadership is a process whereby an organization is effectively influenced by its leaders to achieve goals necessary for its longevity. Influence is the ability to cause desirable and measurable actions and outcomes. Deep leadership influence, our ultimate destination, entails embedding into a structure the DNA that will inevitably bring to fruition the good that we envision.

Social Influence and Genius - A Leadership Journey is not a stereotypical approach as among other things it is manifested in a visual metaphor. The contrast between our method and others is as stark as between the pyramids at Giza and those obscuring the entrance to the Louvre. These methodology of leading others along a similar path. Finally, the highest structure, the Leading or Operating Pyramid, builds a step methodology to reach the company's desired goals and objectives.

The Leadership Trilogy will form a bedrock foundation for building and run one a solid business to challenging times.

This book is like the owner's manual for a car, a detailed...

- Part I -
The Ability to See Through Things

- 1 -
Unlocking the Mystery
The First Pyramid

"You can't change the past, but you can influence the future"

      We stop to rest a moment, like the weary traveler who needs to take a break from the highs and lows of an uneven road. He contemplates the pyramids, and wonders how and why they were made. The mysteries of these great works are still for the most part, unsolved. In your reading you will find rest in understanding what makes a visionary leader effective and enduring. You will unlock the mystery of effectiveness.

The development of leadership ability does not even begin with leadership. It begins with character. The ability to lead is built on it. Every leader leads from his or her character, and, consequently, the shaping of a leader's character is paramount. Leadership means influence and influence roots in character building.

There is nothing more important to P&G's continued success than the development of strong Leaders with the character, values and capabilities required to lead.
> - Robert McDonald, Chairman & CEO, Proctor & Gamble.

As we will see in later chapters, influence has several aspects, some personal, others organizational, and still others transcend the organization. Influence ultimately finds its pinnacle in *Leadership Genius*, as described in its seven actions of chapter 9 (please don't be tempted to skip ahead!).

From the earliest inception of modern social psychology, social influence has been the defining issue. For example, the first experiment in social psychology (Triplett 1898) probed a phenomenon referred to as *social facilitation* —or the tendency for individuals engaging in like behavior to spur on the actions of one another. In this study, Norman Triplett determined that the presence of a competing cyclist upped the level of performance of bicycle riders when compared to their performance levels as they pedaled against the clock. Similarly, Triplett observed school-aged children who were instructed to turn fishing reels as fast as they could. He found that when they worked in pairs, their performance was superior to what it was when they worked alone.

In our leadership journey the approach is in steps. The second step finds its foundation in the first, and the third, in the previous two. This foundational approach forms a natural progression both in understanding and in action. The diagram on the following page illustrates how the steps are laid out in each of the pyramid metaphors. Note that the foundation of the pyramid has four equal sides, and the arrows eventually take you in an upward direction.

We begin with the individual leader. This first pyramid represents leadership development in all of its depth and aspects. The stepwise approach begins at the core of who we are as human persons, and ends with a leader endowed with a new consciousness.

Individual character building is a key objective and closely related to the power of influence and ones level of leadership. In essence, leadership is determined by influence. Either 'learned' or 'born leaders' (as the opinion of some), we are all leaders. Either potentially or active now, every one of us has the power to influence those around us and communicate a better future.

This is achieved in steps (note that character is found in the middle):

    a.   Identity (who I am)
    b.   Values (what I believe)
    c.   Character (where I stand)
    d.   Behavior (what I do)
    e.   Model (what I inspire)

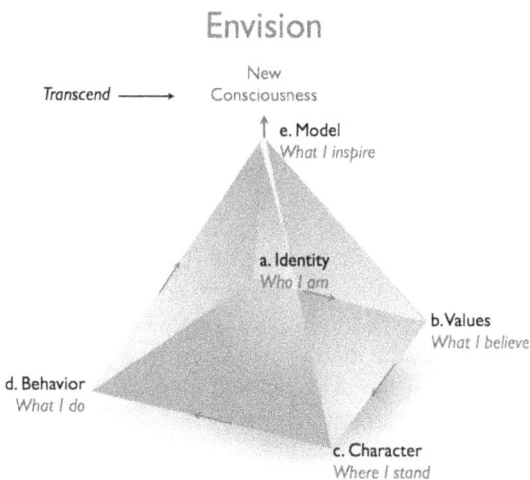

Envision

New
Transcend ⟶ Consciousness

↑ e. Model
What I inspire

a. Identity
Who I am

b. Values
What I believe

d. Behavior
What I do

c. Character
Where I stand

Every step is equally important. Our ultimate goal is to transcend. This term is one of the most important in the book, one that we will revisit over and over as we unlock the mysteries of the pyramids. The term, transcend, is the state of excelling or surpassing the usual limits. In the case of our leader pyramid, transcending is imagined as stretching the pyramid upwards; the base remains the same as the height grows and grows. This upward transcendent motion develops a new consciousness as a leader, and with that, a new vision. This sounds easy, almost trite, but it is far from that. This development requires a life-long journey. The title of this book, *The Leadership Journey – Building Leadership Genius,* expresses well what we hope to accomplish: taking a journey, and building leadership genius.

Our first step, Identity, mostly develops understanding, specifically of ourselves. It can be one of the great stumbling blocks to building leadership genius. The first step toward leadership genius is just as much discovered as acquired. This will become clearer as we move through the book.

A. What makes us human: our interiority and human faculties

Our Interiority

The human person has an incredible ability to know many things. We see, recognize, reflect, and, ultimately, act according to what we have come to know. Man derives this remarkable power to know and reflect because he is a spiritual being. We don't speak about spiritual in the religious sense here, but rather as describing the fundamental makeup of the human person.

To best illustrate this, let's make a visit to the local zoo. Standing at the edge of a monkey's cage, we see the monkey darting about, reacting to every movement in the cage and the overactive school children trying to feed him from the sidewalk. At every instant, the monkey is moved by a perpetual appetite for things that are in the world around him. At every instant, nearby objects and occurrences govern the animal's life. They lead the animal here and there like a marionette doll. An animal does not direct his own existence. It does not live for itself, but rather is continually caught up in what is happening outside itself.

The term interiority describes a defining characteristic of man with respect to animals; what elevates man out of the animal kingdom. Animals lack interiority, causing them to constantly live outside of themselves, fixing their attention on the external world. The attitude of man is different. Although surrounded by the world, human attention is not so absorbed as to prohibit rest and recollection. Man's introspective ability could be described as a radical turning inwards. This turning inwards is where the most important difference between man and animal is found. The activity of thinking or meditating demonstrates man's capacity to stand back from the world and enter into himself, to leave the world behind - to transcend it.

An animal can only know what is to be found in its surroundings and what its senses can grasp; it knows only these trees, or that house. Man, transcending the material environment that surrounds him, grasps the concepts of, all trees, and all houses, because he formulates the idea of tree and the idea of house. This idea goes beyond spatio-temporal limits, that is to say, it is spiritual.

This property, characteristic of man, provides the key to discovering man's very essence. In recognizing this essence, we place ourselves under a spiritual vision of man, rejecting the idea that man is purely material or biological. In affirming the difference between man and animal, we affirm the irreducibility of man to simply another animal. Again, we are not speaking of "spiritual" in the religious sense here. Though, outside the context of this book, this philosophical understanding of "spiritual" could easily form the building blocks necessary to address the concept of "spiritual" from a theological perspective.

Human Faculties
The Intellect

When we speak of human knowledge, we call the human faculty that is able to think and reflect the intellect. The human intellect has an incredible capacity to absorb information. It takes advantage of the human senses of sight, hearing, taste, touch, and smell to gather information, and through abstraction, form universal concepts. The many trees and houses that are around town can form the universal concepts of tree and house. These universal concepts and ideas can exist in themselves, without needing to look at the neighbor's two-story Victorian or the tree your son likes to climb. Not only that, but once these ideas are formed, they can be manipulated to form new entities (think of a centurion, half horse and half man). You won't visibly see a centurion (hopefully!) stopping to eat at the local restaurant, but you could conceive of him having a beer at the local pub.

  The intellect is not only able to form universal ideas, but reflect upon them and form new concepts. In this sense, the intellect is creative; forming new ideas that have their origins in the real world, but take a life of their own within the intellect. The ability of the intellect to meditate on ideas whose origin is in the real world is called *Reditio Completo,* from the Latin for complete reflection. The human intellect has an almost infinite ability to build ideas, one upon the other. The ability to create universal concepts, build new ones, and meditate on them is spiritual. The intellect is a spiritual faculty of the human person. Although the content of ideas finds its origin in the real world, universal concepts, through abstraction and complete reflection, are all spiritual in nature, found only within the intellect.

The Will

  The will is also a faculty of the human person. By will, we mean an act of conscious tendency or desire directed toward an object presented to us by the intellect. In other words, will is acting upon something that we come to know. We cannot desire something that we do not first have knowledge of, and the object of the will is always perceived by the person to be good. By good, we mean that a person believes the object to be attained will benefit them. For example, a man deserted on an island who finds himself hungry for a meal, and fueled by the desire to eat, begins to hunt for food. The hunted animal is seen as good, because it will bring nourishment and fill his belly.

  A counter example is a man who has eaten a five-course meal, and continues to eat another three courses because he likes the taste of the food. The man sees these last courses of food as "a good", but, in fact, they are doing him harm. In all cases, the good is in the eye of the beholder, and in fact, may be harmful. Therefore, the good that we described in this section is a perceived good. We will revisit this topic later, but here we see that the will desires that which is perceived as good, but, to be beneficial, this good must be anchored in truth.

The Heart

If concepts belong to our intellect, and actions and decisions to our will, there is still an element related to the human person that is missing.   Many concepts and decisions are accompanied by an affective charge of fear or hope, joy or sorrow, love or anger, that seem to become so ingrained in us they influence who we are. These feelings or emotions, which accompany our thoughts and actions, are what make our whole being resonate. This is known as the heart. Because feelings and emotions are found both with the intellect and the will they cannot be classified as a human faculty. So where do emotions reside?

They reside in the person, as the subjective part of the experience made by the intellect or the will. For example, in the feeling of sorrow caused by the knowledge of a grave illness, we can distinguish among the cognitive form (the understanding that we are sick, and the cause of that sickness) but also the feeling of sorrow that we have in being in that state. The same can be said about the will. Feelings of anger toward a manager when he or she treats a subordinate unfairly may bring one to visit the manager's office on the person's behalf. This is an act of the will. The emotion of anger accompanying the visit will determine how forcefully we speak out to correct the injustice.

Educating our feels is of great importance in our personal leadership journey. Feeling and emotions can either aid us in reaching our goals or hinder us. They cannot be turned off, but only channeled, and this channeling process requires will power and consistent repetition in order to form habits. Above all, we strive to encourage positive and noble feelings, while directing and limiting the less noble and negative ones. Educating our feeling and emotions must be part of any complete leadership development program.

Management System for our Emotions

Many business leaders take the time and pay the money to further educate themselves. Your average MBA program in the United States costs more than $40,000 a year. Some executives will go back to school after 10 to 15 years in the workforce to get an executive MBA, preparing themselves for greater responsibilities, higher salaries, and job opportunities. These individuals spend their time and money to learn how to better manage money, talent, and to build better strategies. The authors' experience in executive coaching and developing enterprises indicates that executives do not spend enough time and effort managing themselves. There are many examples in corporate America, some of which, unfortunately, reach the front page of the Wall Street Journal. Leaders need to take the time to understand and work diligently to <u>manage themselves</u> more effectively. One of the <u>key components</u> to this is the management of emotions. Good decision-making requires a solid emotional management strategy.

Let's take a moment to think over the past six months. When making decisions that later turned out to have a negative impact on your business, your family life, or within your social network, what went wrong? Take about five minutes to write down the answers to the following questions, for each decision that turned out badly.

1) What was the final result, and could it have been avoided?
2) What was your state of mind at the time, and your emotional state?
3) How could you have managed your emotions better to make a better decision (both at the moment of choosing and the 24 hours prior to this)?

A management System

Let's go a little deeper into question #3 regarding developing a management system. Previously in the book we touched upon the fact that the human person has a spiritual component. Another way to express this is that every person is in fact an "Incarnate Spirit", where we define "incarnate" as to "be embody with" or "invested in a bodily form". This understanding places the emphasis on the spirit, and not the body. The human person is first spiritual, and takes on a body, and not visa versa. Some of the implications for this reality are:

Man as an incarnate spirit
- Man has a body and a spirit, and they are linking together.
- One can profoundly affect the other. The state of our spirit affects our body, and the state of our body effects our spirit.
- The spiritual faculties, the intellect and will, and are closely connected to the functions of our body
- We also have our emotions, and passions (strong emotions) that form part of both our spirit and body.

Our emotions
- Emotions and passions can cloud our judgment and the truth about ourselves
- We can become impulsive by allowing our emotions/passions to direct our lives, rather than reason.
- We can get angry/discouraged when this happens. Anger/discouragement can feed more negative feelings…
- Our physical condition (sleep, diet, exercise) can have a substantial impact on our emotional states and our ability to manage them.

Practical Applications
- We cannot turn off our emotions. They need to be channeled rather than suppressed.
- We need to be aware of our emotional states. When feeling down and out we must be diligent to catch ourselves so that strong negative emotions or thoughts do not enter our head and stay there. We have to have a disciplined spirit. Be especially watchful, self-aware and on top of ourselves.
- We encourage positive and noble feelings, and channel and limit the less noble and negative feelings
- What is a negative feeling? Those that lead us down the wrong path and away from the truth about ourselves… that is to say, thoughts that do not have their basis in an

<u>optimistic understanding of ourselves and the world around us</u>, those which are selfish, pessimistic, that do not reflect the faith and value system that we live by.

- Daydreaming when we are tired or fatigued can lead to negative feelings and thoughts.
- Diligence when we are sleepy is helpful, keeping busy and well scheduled. Getting out of bed with the first ring of the alarm clock helps to strengthen ourselves.
- Having an full schedule, being well organized and planning our day are of great benefit.
- Form the <u>habit of watchfulness</u> and action when unhealthy thoughts and feelings enter our lives. We do not suppress those feelings, but channel them, catching ourselves when they arrive. Lack of sleep and exercise can have a strong affect on our ability to do this.
- Watch with serenity. We don't control of what enters are heads. When negative thoughts arrive we simply set them aside, not letting them take hold, carrying off our peace of mind.
- <u>We are weak and fragile by our nature, not our choice</u>. We cannot allow negative thoughts and feelings to get us down. We do nothing wrong because of what enters our head.
- We need to appreciate the faith, and value system that we have received. This is fundamental to our serenity and the educating of our emotions.
- We must avoid useless lamenting about things that could have been. We accept the things that come our way and make the very best of them.
- Ruminating over and over about the downsides and disappointments of our lives will carry us downward, spiraling our emotions out of control.

Go Deeper   www.effective-leadership.com/go-deeper

B. How we measure (know) ourselves: assessments

In our discussion of the first pyramid, we focus our attention on a stepwise approach to building the visionary, effective and enduring leader. Our first step has been looking at one's identity (who I am). We have, from a philosophical perspective, touched upon the core of the human person (their interiority, spiritual nature, intellect, will, and heart). We call this study anthropology (from the Greek *antros*- man, and *ology*- the study of), or the study of man.

Is there a way to accurately measure aspects of our identity, to qualify and quantify, at least to a partial extent "who I am". Yes. We accomplish this through assessments. The science of assessments has matured a great deal over the past 30 years. Assessments are tools, usually in the form of a series of questions to answer or problems to solve. The subject provides information that opens the door to key insights into the core of the individual. There are many types of assessments, some that are excellent, others that are very poor. The key to finding a good family of assessments is to review their foundational principles, and their validation. Their foundational principles must be in harmony with a solid anthropology (understanding of man at his/her core) as we discussed above. The danger here, as in anything else, is that erroneous beginnings will provide skewed or meaningless results at the end.

Secondly, the assessments must be validated, that is to say, what the assessment is predicting about behavior must match the subjects behavior in real world. To validate these tests there must be years and years of data collected from those who have taken the assessment. This data is then fed back into the system to validate and improve the test itself. It often takes 20-25 years of data to provide this level of validation, with qualified statisticians and other experts doing the work. Relatively few assessments achieve this level of robustness.

The chart shown here describes the four families of assessments and what they measure from an anthropological perspective. The box of the far right, Effectiveness, indicates that the sum total of the four boxes to its left add up to the overall effectiveness of the person, as measured by these types of tests.

Understanding Assessment

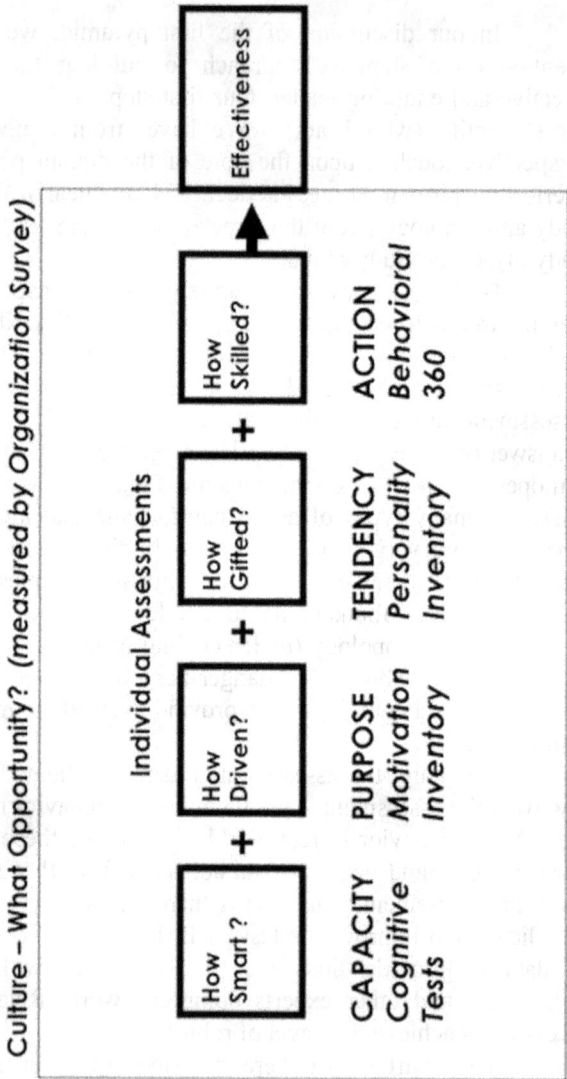

Culture – What Opportunity? *(measured by Organization Survey)*

Individual Assessments

How Smart?	How Driven?	How Gifted?	How Skilled?
CAPACITY Cognitive Tests	PURPOSE Motivation Inventory	TENDENCY Personality Inventory	ACTION Behavioral 360

→ Effectiveness

Chart courtesy of *Dr Paul M. Connolly, Ph.D*
Performance Programs Inc

Capacity, or IQ, is the measure of intelligence. We are all familiar with IQ tests, and they have been standardized over the years. Ones' IQ does not change over time. Once the mind develops in our youth (until we are about 10 years old), our IQ is set for life. We can consider this aspect of our core to be part of how we are hardwired. IQ is something we have, not something we learn or acquire. As we will see later on, the same is true of personality. Studies show, that among senior executives, IQ is generally within the same range, on the upper side of the scale. This becomes clear when we think about all that it takes to arrive at a senior level position (graduate studies, demonstrated ability to find solutions to complex issues etc.). This tends to level the playing field with regards to IQ, so executives must stand out as effective in other areas (e.g. personality, relational skills, and intuition).

The second box in our diagram, labeled purpose, is a measure of one's motivation or drive. The drive that you possess in reaching a role is of great importance, because reaching a desired outcome often requires overcoming difficult obstacles. The measure of How Driven is the measure of momentum, or force, behind the desire. We discussed earlier the tendency of the human will toward that which it sees as good. How good something is will be determined by a number of factors, but in particular our values system. Later in the chapter we will discuss in detail how our motives and drives are linked to our values. We measure personal drive with what is called a motive inventory, an assessment that measures what moves us toward attaining a desired outcome.

The third section on the diagram, labeled tendency, is a measure of our personality. Personality is developed during our early childhood. By the age of five or six, our personality is for the most part set in stone. We can measure personality in our teens, middle age, and other times in our life and it will not change. Our personality, like our IQ, is how we are hardwired. Personality is the expression of ourselves, as we are. Traumatic experiences in the early years, when personality is formed, can have very negative consequences when we are older, such as personality disorders. We must note here that personality is both a consequence of genetics and early childhood rearing. The word tendency is used to describe personality because how we behave does not rest solely on our personality. We have a natural tendency to act particular ways, or pattern of behavior, based on our personality, but we may act differently, through self-awareness and training. If we were to let ourselves go, and follow our natural tendency, we would behave very much as our personality dictates. For example, someone can, by nature or personality, be quite shy, but faced with a particular opportunity (like getting a promotion), come out of themselves to perform in a different manner (becoming assertive or even bold). The expression of our personality depends not only on our nature, but our values and our motivations as well.

The fourth box in the diagram, labeled "action" is a measure of how others see us. Of the four types of measurement of ourselves that we have covered, this is the only one where other people rather than ourselves do the evaluation. This assessment, known as a 360 degree test, bases itself on inquiries made to your boss, colleagues, subordinates, and even clients about your leadership style, collaborative drive, and communication skills. Often we find a disconnect between how we perceive ourselves and how others perceive us. We may think of ourselves as relatively patient, understanding, and trusting, while a subordinate may look upon us as someone who is overbearing and likes to micromanage our work.

Measuring these four areas: our intelligence (how smart), our motivation (how driven), personality (how gifted), and behavior (how skilled) can bring us some deep insights into ourselves, and the path we need to take to grow in our leadership and effectiveness.

Personality

Understanding our personality, in detail, is paramount to growing as a leader. Uncovering our hardwiring will open our eyes to understanding what we can change, what is inherently part of us, and how we can channel our motivations toward personal success. The well-known serenity prayer says it well; "God grant me the serenity to accept the things I cannot change; courage to change the things I can; and wisdom to know the difference". Let's take a brief look at the aspects that are often measured in determining personality.

Scale	Description
Adjustment	Concerns composure, optimism, and stable moods.
Ambition	Concerns taking initiative, being competitive, and seeking leadership roles.
Sociability	Concerns seeming talkative, socially bold, and entertaining.
Interpersonal Sensitivity	Concerns being agreeable, considerate, and skilled at maintaining relationships.
Prudence	Concerns being conscientious, dependable, and rule-abiding.
Inquisitive	Concerns being curious, imaginative, visionary, and easily bored.
Learning Approach	Concerns enjoying formal education and actively staying up-to-date on business and technical matters.

Description above from Hogan HPI. Assessments scales mentioned in this chapter and the next are from Hogan Assessment Systems, one of the leading personality profiling systems, and most used among Fortune 500 companies.

The key to understanding this type of assessment is discovering how personality traits combine. Note that the terms above (adjustment, ambition etc.) should be understood in the context of how they are defined above, and not the commonplace definition of the word.

> Executives are often hired for their competency (resume, skills) and fired for their personality!

Let's take an example of a CEO that we recently worked with. After taking the test, we reviewed the results and found that his adjustment scale was in the 25th percentile, his sociability the 85th percentile, and his interpersonal sensitivity in the 40th percentile. A low adjustment score means that the person tends to be opposite what is described above (composed, optimistic and stable moods). He is in fact quite emotional, tends to be moody, and angers easily. A high sociability score tells us that this individual enjoys social settings and tends to gravitate toward them (a social butterfly). A low interpersonal sensitivity score tells us that he is direct and to the point, but has difficulty relating to others' needs and their situations (lacks compassion and has a hard time putting himself in their shoes). The result, an individual that is emotionally volatile, tends to spend a lot of time with people, but lacks the skills to relate to them, may often alienate others, is very direct, and lacks compassion. Would this be someone you would like to work for?

A great deal of research has been done on personality, and much evidence points to the fact that people with certain combinations of personality traits are more suited to certain jobs than others. This has been shown to be true in researching thousands of individuals as they perform their various functions in the workplace.

We can identify a number of job families, where personality is often an important role in performance: Managers and Executives; Professionals; Technicians and Specialists; Operations and Trades; Sales and Customer Support; Administration and Clerical; Service and Support. Let's look at the example of Sales and Customer Support.

The Sales and Customer Support job family consists of jobs that require the employee to build the credibility of the organization through social interaction and to establish long lasting relationships with clients. Examples include sales executives, telemarketers, customer service representatives, and account managers. If the target job fits this description, look for the following pattern in the personality profile: average to high Ambition and Prudence, and average Adjustment and Interpersonal Sensitivity. This is the profile of a person who is competitive, and self-assured (Ambition) and dependable and organized (Prudence). This person will also be even-tempered (Adjustment) while also possessing an appropriate sense of urgency. This person will be friendly and cooperative (Interpersonal Sensitivity), but able to handle conflict appropriately.

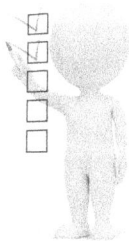

We have been amazed by how much personality effects job performance and job fit. We can look at a job family, review the specific job description of a position in a particular company, and create an ideal personality profile for the position. The success rate using this as a tool for selecting candidates has been very successful. Here is one dramatic example:

A Case Study – Increased Annual Sales

An international manufacturer of fragrances used in perfumes and cosmetics wanted to improve the selection of successful sales representatives. Hogan used the HPI and HDS to identify individuals best suited to perform in these challenging sales roles. Our review of sales performance data showed a favorable long-term trend, such that, as profile fit improved, performance increased. Specifically, individuals who did not meet the profile had annual sales revenue of $875,000, whereas those who did meet the combined HPI and HDS profile delivered much stronger sales ($4,000,000).

Derailers – Personality under pressure

Too much of a good thing can have negative consequences. This is particularly true with regards to personality. Excessive attention to detail can lead to micromanaging. Keeping to the rules and following the playbook too closely can lead to being inflexible and lacking creativity. Being imaginative without regard for practicality can lead people to perceive you as eccentric and out in left field.

Derailers are aspects of our personality that show themselves when we are particularly stressed, fatigued, or frustrated. The structure of the human person is such that these pressures need an outlet, like a pressure cooker on the stove needs to let out steam or it will eventually explode. When we let off stream through our personality it can negatively affect our relationships with others.

We must note that our discussion here speaks of a hardwired response to pressure, not a bad attitude or negative disposition. This makes it easier to understand why certain people act in ways that may annoy us over and over, though they may never directly intend to be bothersome. It is easier to forgive a spouse or friend for negative behavior under pressure and fatigue when we become aware that this behavior comes more from their nature than attitude. How much more forgiving could we be when what we thought was a spouse's bad disposition was in fact an expression of their personality (under pressure). This is not to say that we cannot recognize and control these responses. The combination of a positive upbringing, self-awareness, and self-discipline can go a long way to channel these tendencies.

Below is a list of derailers used to measure an executive's personality under pressure. It must be noted here that executives are under stress much of the time, so these may manifest themselves more than infrequently.

Scale	Description
Excitable	Concerns being overly enthusiastic about people/projects, and then becoming disappointed with them
Skeptical	Concerns being socially insightful, but cynical and overly sensitive to criticism
Cautious	Concerns being overly worried about being criticized
Reserved	Concerns lacking interest in or awareness of the feelings of others
Leisurely	Concerns being charming, but independent, stubborn, and hard to coach

Bold	Concerns having inflated views of one's competency and worth
Mischievous	Concerns being charming, risk-taking, and excitement-seeking
Colorful	Concerns being dramatic, engaging, and attention seeking
Imaginative	Concerns thinking and acting in interesting, unusual, and even eccentric ways
Diligent	Concerns being conscientious, perfectionistic, and hard to please
Dutiful	Concerns being eager to please and reluctant to act independently

Above from Hogan Assessment System HDS profile

Assessments that utilize these scales are used both for leadership development (within the context of executive coaching, team building activities, and off-site retreats) as well as in evaluating candidates for hire. Many Fortune 500 companies use these tools to gain deeper insight into candidates (far beyond what can be learned from the standard interview process). Regarding derailers, high-risk jobs such as firemen, policemen, nuclear plant operators, etc. are of particular interest. Then again, any senior executive under stress can be dangerous! Employers need to hire people that can handle stress well. It would not be prudent to hire an individual as an inner-city policeman who has the tendency to fly off the handle in anger when under pressure. He or she may put him/herself and others at risk of bodily harm. The United States military uses these types assessments extensively for selecting personal for high-pressure/high-risk positions such as fighter pilots and covert operations. Measuring personality under pressure is a key indicator of how individuals will cope with high-risk situations.

The authors of this book have provided valuable insights to company leadership in hiring for senior positions (such as CEOs or CFOs). Many people at this level are excellent interviewers, but may not be good managers or solid leaders. Providing deep insight into personality, personal values (for cultural fit), and derailers can save search committees and company boards many future headaches. A quick review of the average tenure (about 18 months) of Fortune 2000 company leaders indicates that there is a particular need for hiring wisely. The monetary loss (not to mention the loss to the company's momentum) of hiring and rehiring company leaders is astronomical.

Go
Deeper   www.effective-leadership.com/go-deeper

- 2 -
Transcending

"To thine own self be true"
William Shakespeare

In chapter one we learned about the human person, whose nature has the unique qualities of interiority and a spiritual dimension. We also discovered how intelligence and personality are hard-wired within us, forming part of who we are, unchanged during our lifetime. Now we continue our journey, as we build our leader pyramid and learn about other aspects of ourselves that can change and develop over time. Leadership is a lifelong journey that requires effort and self-awareness.

Our ultimate goal is to transcend the usual limits as a leader in order to reach new heights, both personally and professionally. In our first pyramid, based on the stepwise approach of building one core principle on another, we look at: values, character, behavior, and model leadership.

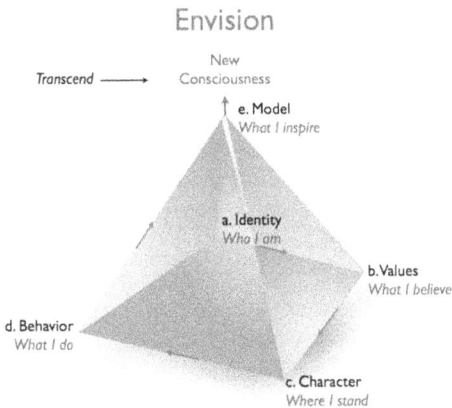

Envision

Transcend ⟶ New Consciousness

e. Model
What I inspire

a. Identity
Who I am

b. Values
What I believe

d. Behavior
What I do

c. Character
Where I stand

Values (what I believe)

The word "values" is used often in ethics discussions. We can define values as "a principle, standard, or quality considered worthwhile or desirable". We all, in one form or another, abide by a system of values. What each individual or group sees as worthwhile or desirable can vary greatly. The key ingredients to living within a personal system of values are: clarity, conviction, and consistency.

A. **Clarity** – Understanding what one believes in, with crystal clear precision, with the ability to articulate those values verbally and in writing. Recently, during a talk at a luncheon for small business owners, the group was asked to write down the top five values that governed their actions day to day in their businesses. Many were not able to put the list together on paper with ease. They simply could not articulate their beliefs.

B. **Conviction** – the ability to apply one's core values with energy and precision, regardless of the obstacles, personal discomfort, or apparent dangers.

C. **Consistency** – the constant application of one's values or beliefs over time, according to an appropriate hierarchy of values. A hierarchy of values prioritizes our beliefs by transcendence when one is in conflict with another.

Let's now examine how our personal values interact with those of a group. To aid in our discussion, we can further define a value system: *The accepted mode of conduct and the set of norms, goals, and values binding any social group that serves as a frame of reference for the individual in reaching decisions and achieving a meaningful life.*

Here, the harmony or compatibility between our personal value system and those of the group (corporate, social, or church environment) can greatly impact our ability to thrive in those particular surroundings. Think about the executive who goes to work each day, wanting to get up in the morning, commute across town, and work extra hours. What makes his work environment a place he or she wants to spend most of his waking moments? It is the harmony and compatibility between his or her personal values and those in the workplace.

The norms, goals, and values that surround us in the workplace serve as a frame of reference for making decisions. We can call this environment corporate culture. Think of the culture at your workplace. What are the norms and values that serve as your framework for making a decision? Does the environment encourage you to think outside the box? Does it reward you for personal initiative? Or, are the corporate mores encouraging you to follow the rulebook very closely?

Measuring our values

We saw in the first chapter that assessment can help us measure our motives and values. Let's take a closer look at one of these assessments, called the Motives, Values, and Preferences Inventory. This test helps us understand what motivates and moves us, day to day.

Scale	Description
Aesthetics	Interest in the look, feel, sound, and design of products and artistic work.
Affiliation	Need for frequent and varied social contact.
Altruistic	Desire to serve others, to improve society, and to help the less fortunate.
Commerce	Interest in earning money, realizing profits, and finding business opportunities.
Hedonism	Desire for fun, excitement, variety, and pleasure.
Power	Desire for challenge, competition, achievement, and success.
Recognition	Desire to be known, seen, visible, and famous.
Science	Interest in new ideas, technology, and a rational, data-based approach to problem solving.
Security	Need for structure, order, and predictability.
Tradition	Concerns for morality, family values, and devotion to duty.

Above from Hogan Assessment System MVPI profile

Taking advantage of an assessment of what moves us to action, such as this one, can help us learn a great deal about ourselves. Take, for example, the measure called recognition, or the desire to be known, seen, visible, and famous. For many individuals in business, being recognized for accomplishments is very important (admitting it publically is another question altogether). Recognition for a job well done is encouraging, and stimulates greater self-confidence and esteem. Take a sales director who receives companywide recognition for reaching the sales goal for the quarter. He will be driven to do even better next quarter. Compare this to the culture of an organization that does not give any praise or recognition to this same sales executive. Over time, this lack of recognition becomes an issue for the individual.

Research has shown that when there are three or more disconnects or gaps between company cultural values and personal employee values listed above, the retention rate for employees drops considerably. We have seen over and over how companies with these disconnects have a very difficult time with employee turnover, at all levels of their organizations.

<u>Core values</u>

Our research, taken from experience working with senior executives and their organizations for many years, has led us to identify 12 core values that are essential to success, both individually and collectively. Training in the incorporation of these values is essential to helping executives grow in leadership. The majority of larger organizations outline a set of core values on paper, usually on their website, in literature, or as part of their annual report. Relatively few, however, have been successful in this. The first and last of the core values below are shown in detail, the rest can be seen reviewed online by visiting the *Go Deeper* section of this book.

<u>Business</u>

Excellence
The pursuit of distinction in business, family, and community
- Insists on excellence in all things and sets the example

- Provides recognition beyond wins and billability
- Makes objective, quality service to the client a top priority; sets the example
- Continuously strives to improve work processes, products, and services
- Provides timely effective, accurate, and constructive performance feedback to team
- Recruits and develops quality staff with potential
- Contributes to and stays current with developments in the field

Teamwork
Mutual collaboration to reach common objectives without focus on personal again

Entrepreneurship
Turning opportunity into success through prudent action

Service
Adding value through conscience effort and personal leadership

Diversity
Appreciation for the value of differences

Influence
Moving others to think and act uprightly through conscious effort

Individual

Professionalism
Empowering self and others to maximize effectiveness

Fairness
Giving others their due in word and deed

Integrity
Consistency between what one professes to be and how one lives

Respect
Esteeming others by extending the same courtesy with which one hopes to be afforded

Trust
Building confidence through insightful action

Self-Mastery
Controlling one's passions amid personal drive
- Exercises self-constraint in times of strong passions
- Delays words and actions when excited to anger, frustration, or discouragement
- Steps back from situations when compelling, strong emotions are present in others.

Go
Deeper
www.effective-leadership.com/go-deeper

Character (Where I stand)

On a personal level, how do we express our values? Our values are both convictions of the mind, and actions of the heart expressed in and through words. Our actions, that is to say, our behaviors are available for everyone to observe. Our leadership is expressed through our behavior.

A habit is formed through repetitive behavior. Think of it like a cart pushed down a hill, day after day after day. Initially the cart swerves back and forth, in a zigzag fashion, until it reaches the bottom. But, after a few days, a ridge begins to form in the earth, and the path of the cart begins to stabilize. After a week or so, the cart follows the same path over and over with ease. So it is with many of our actions. We form habits, and our behaviors stabilize, taking on the same form over and over. Therefore, how I acted yesterday effects how I will act today and tomorrow (like the cart that begins following the path etched in the earth during the previous days). We form dispositions that affect our future. Our behaviors are not autonomous – one action completely independent from the previous; rather, they are linked to one another.

This brings us to the question of character. Character is the acquired disposition related to forming habits, formed in us when we repeat actions over and over. This creates a disposition or tendency in us to lean one way or another. Positive acts provide good habits, while negative acts produce bad habits. Virtue is formed in us when we choose to do positive actions, over and over, creating a disposition to move in the positive direction. The same is true of vice for the negative.

Let's take an example from Physics 101. Newton's Law states that an object in motion tends to stay in motion unless acted on by a force. So it is with character. You build up momentum in one direction or the other. Moving in the opposite direction requires that you slow down, bring the momentum to zero, change direction, and begin to speed up in the opposite direction. To break a bad habit and form a good one requires this changing of direction. It is not easy.

Behavior

In short, behavior is the sum total of everything that we have seen so far. Behavior is comprised of our Identity (who I am), values (what I believe), and character (where I stand, and lean). Who we are is a combination of nature and nurture. Our Identity, or natural tendency, is unchanging. Part of the wisdom we must acquire, day by day, is how to distinguish between what is nature (fixed) and what is changeable (nurture). We go back to the Serenity prayer, "God grant me the serenity to accept the things I cannot change, the courage to change the things I can, and the wisdom to know the difference".

This wisdom comes in understanding ourselves well, so that we can build on what we already are. Leadership is a lifelong journey that begins at the moment we wake up each morning.

The Personal Business Plan

Building leadership requires planning and concerted effort. The personal business plan is just as it sounds: a business plan, but applied to oneself personally rather than to one's company. It is a means of transforming your behavior, based on all that we have seen so far. We can define a company business plan as follows:

> A business plan is a document that summarizes the operational and financial objectives of a business and contains the detailed plans and budgets showing how the objectives are to be realized. It often describes the nature of the business, the sales and marketing strategy, the financial background, and contains a projected profit and loss statement.

The personal business plan does the same, but the focus is not on the business directly, but on the individual leader. It summarizes the operational and personal objectives of leadership and contains detailed plans of how the objectives are to be realized. The *Personal Business Plan* is a tested tool for making your time investment yield maximum returns. It helps you identify the real causes of your successes and failures, and it fuels excellence in business and in your personal life. Here is an overview of the plan:

- Executive Assessment (mentioned in this chapter and the previous one)
  o Personality
  o Motives and Drivers
  o Derailers
- Core Value Assessment
  o An assessment based on the core values mentioned earlier in this chapter
- Personal SWOT Analysis
- Roll Out of Goals & Objectives
- Key Performance Indicators (KPI)
- Follow-up

A survey of 140 leading executive coaches conducted by Harvard Business Review found that the reasons companies engage coaches have changed. Ten years ago, most companies called coaches in to help fix toxic behavior at the top. Today, most coaching aims to develop the capabilities of top performers.

- Harvard Business School Journal, January 2009

Traditionally the Personal Business Plan is developed over four or five sessions with an executive coach. The resulting document is the action plan, and the leader and coach work together to implement it. The coach becomes an accountability partner for the executive. The most important aspect of the plan is ownership by the leader of the goals and objectives.

Building a habit of self-reflection is an important part of this entire process. In order to understand ones motives, drives, and intentions, a habit of daily self-analysis and reflection is invaluable. This has traditionally been known as a personal 'examination of conscience'. Taking a few minutes aside each day to think and meditate on our goals, intentions, and actions helps us listen to our inner self, and follow the built in compass known as our conscience. How many leaders have failed because they did not turn to this inner compass for guidance.

Go
Deeper   www.effective-leadership.com/go-deeper

Executive Coaching

Coaching can be of great value for an executive seeking to better his or her performance by influencing those around him or her to perform better. The authors of this book have seen breakthrough advances in organizations where individual leaders, with the help of executive coaching, refocused and recommitted themselves to the top priorities of the company. A recent example for us was CEO of a fast growth Oil and Gas Exploration Company, who, through a greater self-awareness of leadership gaps, re-invented himself, rebuilt his executive team, and outran the competition in just two years.

Some of the important qualities to look for in executive coaches are:

- Strong general business acumen
- At least 10 years of experience as an executive coach
- A passion for helping others advance their leadership
- Deep understanding of the mechanics of the human person based on foundational principles (similar to those outlined in chapters one and two).

Model (what I inspire)

Our true value as a leader is our capacity to influence others. Many books have been written about how to be an inspiring leader. The authors of this book know that being a model leader begins deep within us. We have taken the steps: Identity, Values, Character, and Behavior. Being a model leader is where we begin to transcend who we are as individuals, and multiply ourselves. This is the essence of leadership genius. Leaders rally people toward a better future. They can't help but change the present, because the present isn't good enough. Success happens when they find a way to make people excited by and confident in what comes next.

Leadership is not something that you do at work, but not at home, or on the weekends with friends. True leadership is 24/7, in all environments and at all moments. We lead by example. They say that "actions speak louder than words", but sometimes your actions are speaking so loudly, I can hardly hear you!

Transcending as aligning

Leadership genius is about transcending as a leader. A way to better understanding this important fact is to think of transcending as aligning (ordering to each other) the various aspects of being a leader that we have seen so far.

a. Identity (who I am)
b. Values (what I believe)
c. Character (where I stand)
d. Behavior (what I do)
e. Model (what I inspire)

Take for example if our values are not aligned with our behavior. We may believe strongly in something yet our behavior may not reflect this (they are misaligned). A man has a strong belief in treating others with respect and defending their reputations when the other person is not present (a value for him), yet at the water cooler bad mouths his colleagues just like everyone else (behavior does not align). As we will discover in the next chapter, the same holds true for qualities of solid team building.

TRANSCEND ⟵⟶ ALIGN

Transcend ⟶ Underachieve

Align   Diverge

Leadership Styles

Part of leadership genius is being all things to all men so that all may benefit from the leader's vision. Each of us has a way of working, relating to others, delegating tasks etc., but it is not enough to rely on our inner resources within our comfort zone, or in conformity with our personality. *As leaders, we must adapt.*

Leadership is less about *your* needs, and more about the needs of the people and the organization you are leading. Strong leaders adapt to the particular demands of the situation and the people involved, taking into account the particular challenges facing the organization.

One of Daniel Goleman's most accomplished works, *Primal Leadership*, describes six different styles of leadership. The most effective leaders are able to move among these styles, adopting the one that meets the needs of the moment. As you review these think about moments in your business and personal life where changing your leadership style would have produced a better result.

Visionary

The visionary style of leadership works best when an organization needs a new direction or needs to be revitalized, awoken from slumber. Its goal is to move people toward a new set of shared dreams. "Visionary leaders articulate where a group is going, but not how it will get there – setting people free to innovate, experiment, take calculated risks," writes Mr. Goleman and his coauthors.

Coaching

This style involves a one-on-one focus for developing individuals, enlightening the path to improving their performance, and helping to connect their personal and professional goals to those of the organization. Coaching works best, Mr. Goleman writes, "with employees who show initiative and want more professional development." There is a negative side to this if it is perceived as micromanaging, or simply collecting information about an employee's performance and/or attitudes. The key here is that the leader authentically desires to help the other to improve.

Affiliative

This style emphasizes the importance of teamwork, building unity and harmony in a group by connecting people to each other. Mr. Goleman suggests that this approach is particularly valuable "when trying to heighten team harmony, increase morale, improve communication or repair broken trust in an organization." Goleman also notes that in using this style alone may have a negative side because it leaves unchecked poor individual performance "Employees may perceive," he writes, "that mediocrity is tolerated." As mentioned earlier, a strong leader uses a number of styles to counterbalance negative and positive effects.

Democratic

This style relies on people's knowledge and skill set, and creates a group commitment to the resulting goals. Goleman says that this style works best when the organizations direction needs refocused, where the leader needs to tap into the collective wisdom of the group. Mr. Goleman suggests that this consensus-building approach may produce negative results in times of crisis or upheaval, when urgent events demand quick decisions. Consensus building must have a strong leader at the helm, one that knows how to facilitate dialogue, consolidate options, and defuse negativity.

Pacesetting

In the pacesetting style the leader sets high standards of performance and demands results from others. Many leaders take this approach on a daily basis, driving desired results with energy, and inviting other to higher standards. Mr. Goleman warns this style should be used sparingly, because it can undercut morale and make people feel as if they are failing. "Our data shows that, more often than not, pacesetting poisons the climate," he writes.

Commanding

This command and control model is the most used, but often the least effective. "I want results, and if I can't get them from you, I will look to others to find them." This style rarely involves rewarding the positive, and often implies fear of failure for underperformers. This style undercuts morale and job satisfaction. Mr. Goleman argues it is only effective in a crisis, when an urgent turnaround is needed. The modern military has come to recognize its limited usefulness.

From Daniel Goleman's Book, "Primal Leadership" published by Harvard Business Press, 2002.

Extensive research has shown that each of these styles is effective, and needs to be applied according to the need at hand.

- Part II -
The Ability to See Things Through

- 3 -
Basics
Feed a Culture

*"In any great company – it's not about a great individual leader,
it's about a leadership culture in the company"*
-- James Owens, former Chairman and CEO Caterpillar

Practically every long-lived and highly successful
company attributes the primary source of its prosperity to its
culture - not its smart leaders, not its technology, not its superior
strategies, but its culture. This is true for General Electric,
Hewlett-Packard, Southwest Airlines, Cisco Systems, Disney,
Starbucks, and countless others. Culture is important because it is
the source from which an organization operates. Culture involves
every aspect of the organization: how it is designed, how people
relate to one another, what is considered to be true, what is
deemed important, the criteria to use for decisions, how to treat
customers, and a myriad of other factors.

As a leader, how would you like to create a culture of
excellence, where your people serve the customers with passion
and serve each other with respect? Would you like to have a
culture where the team works together to achieve common goals
and each employee consistently strives to get better; where smiles
and positive attitudes are the norm and not the exception? Some
years ago one of the authors was visiting a large corporation and
rode the elevator up several floors with a group of employees just
coming to work. He noticed that everyone was looking down at
their feet and not greeting one another, or even talking at all. We
later found out that their actions were indicative of their less than

robust corporate culture, as well as the corporation's mediocre business performance.

There are many definitions of culture, but most agree that it refers to a system of shared assumptions, values, and norms that define appropriate attitudes and behaviors for its members. Culture is a multi-layered tapestry of values and norms. Much of a company's cultural assumptions and norms are inherited from its industry, from the overall economy, and from society. These inherited assumptions and norms are practically invisible to most companies because they are simply accepted as truths, i.e. the basic operating and design assumptions. This makes them very difficult to change and explains why cultural lock-in can be so pernicious.

Organizational culture can be compared to the operating system on your computer. An operating system, such as Windows or Unix, determines what software can be run on your computer and how it will be run (slow or fast, which features are supported, etc.). If you are running the DOS operating system today, there is very little software available that will run on your computer. Likewise with culture, if you want to perform an activity that is not supported by the culture, it will fail. It does not matter how hard you try to perform the activity or how committed you are to its success; it will not succeed until you change or align with the underlying "cultural operating system".

For instance, the business media reports that the majority of recent ERP (Enterprise Resource Planning) software system implementations have failed to meet expectations. ERP systems require a high level of integration among functional areas. Many companies have a long history of silos and independence among their functional groups. As a result, their cultural operating systems could not support the level of collaboration needed for success. In these cases, ignoring the cultural issues contributed significantly to the ERP system's failure.

Try this for perspective: culture is how you currently operate in the following 7 areas.

1. **Ethics**: the dominant characteristics of the organization
2. **Risk**: the explicit values at the foundation of decisions and actions
3. **Trust**: the dominant work environment

4. **Accountability**: the unwritten performance expectations
5. **Integrity**: the specific behaviors that are valued
6. **Alignment**: leaders who walk the walk
7. **Rewards**: the criteria of success people are evaluated by

An interesting blog we came across addressed the strength of a culture in a unique way. Efforts to improve performance usually fail because too often the change is at odds with the culture. When change is at odds with culture, culture will always win. If you can't change the hearts and minds, (the values, ways of thinking approaches to problems, management styles, and motivations), the culture soon adopts resistance to change as a coping mechanism and defaults to staying the same. To change the culture is awkward, self-conscious, and complex. It's better to avoid it if possible. Peter Drucker is often quoted as saying, "company cultures are like country cultures. Never try to change one. Try, instead, to work with what you've got."

A recent study of corporate culture and KM (Knowledge Management) initiatives (McDermott and O'Dell, 2000) found that however strong the commitment and approach to knowledge management may be, culture is stronger. Companies successful at sharing knowledge did not try to change their culture to fit their Knowledge Management approach. They build their Knowledge Management approach to fit their culture. They describe Knowledge Management as a way to enable people to pursue something that the organization and its members already value. This makes sharing knowledge a more natural step that requires less convincing than a direct change campaign.

Strengthening Your Culture

Wholesale cultural shifts are impractical and undesirable. The goal is to purposefully shape your culture over time, building on the attributes of your current culture that you want to retain. Jim Bethmann of Caldwell Partners International uses the analogy of feeding the beast, or offering a healthy diet versus an unhealthy one, to feed (strengthen) a culture. You feed the culture or provide a healthy diet by choosing mid-performers (or processes...) and moving them into high performance mode. Most businesses are made up of average people and processes. We often have a few great performers and a few poor ones. They tend to balance each other out to make an average business. Many businesses get trapped in being average. Average is a state where we are comfortable, and maybe even satisfied. But in reality it's a state where we know we can do better. Getting to the next level has challenges we may not understand or be willing to tackle on our own, so apathy sets in and our competition moves on.

You must fortify your company values. Most firms have a formally identified set of core values. But there are wide differences in the degree to which these espoused values actually impact their respective organizations. Since shared values constitute the foundation of your culture, this is an important step to strengthening your culture. You have to go beyond merely posting them on the wall or talking about them; they have to be lived out. Research on the subject clearly indicates that even during an economic crisis, the performance of companies with adaptive and flexible cultures is markedly better financially when compared to companies with a poorly defined and inflexible work culture. Every organization has its own brand of culture that evolves over time and is based on values and vision that are unique to that organization. This cannot be overlooked on the path to success. It should rather be addressed in the organization's vision, goal statements, training, and communication.

Align Business Values with Individual Values

The vision and values of an organization help to keep it on track toward a common goal shared by all individuals. Decisions cannot be made on business values alone. A corporation must be willing to examine their values and review if or how they align with the values of their people.

Research shows that when the values of employees are in alignment with the values of an organization (the leader's values) the organization is more successful and more focused on customer satisfaction and community service. Organizations that do not have this alignment tend to be bureaucratic, stressful, and even toxic places to work. They may be financially successful but find it difficult to hire and keep self-motivated and talented people. Companies with aligned values have very few problems attracting and retaining talented people. They know what their employees want and they know how to provide it.

An organization with an overly political, stressful, and toxic culture will drive away good people with solid values and cost millions. A values disconnect, in its simplest form, can be measured by turnover: 51% of all top performers are actively looking for another job! What would losing 1 or 2 of your best people cost your organization?

One of the best recent examples of leading an organization with a fractious culture to success is Ford CEO Alan Mulally, an auto-outsider who has taken Ford from near bankruptcy to a global leadership position. His levelheaded leadership (he developed a clear point of view and an operating plan, then *aligned the* culture with the plan) put the carmaker back on the road to financial stability.

Two interesting findings came from a study by Dr. Rob Cook from Human Synergistics International. He measured the correlation between profit margin and how constructive the culture of the organization was.

A constructive culture is one where there is a sense of achievement, challenge, growth, encouragement, and humanistic relationships. The first conclusion was that organizations with a constructive culture sustained higher profit margins. In fact, the more constructive the culture, the higher the profit margin and the more stable the profit over time.

In order to build a truly great company, we must find the medium place, slightly more than just taking care of business, yet slightly less than a company religion. There has to be a strong positive influence structure that results in a requisite culture.

The culture starts with the people who have a fantastic cultural fit, are strong leaders, have proven ability to perform their roles, and will do it at one hundred miles per hour.

To build a high performance workplace, you must find new employees, when needed that can compliment and raise the skill set and effectiveness of the entire group. A business' hiring process is just like building a sports team. You need to bring in those that can improve the team. A football team never considers bringing in players just to fill out the team. Rather, they obsess about bringing in players that will help win the Super Bowl trophy.

All champion teams have a strong cultural environment. Your company should be structured the same way.

Go Deeper

www.effective-leadership.com/go-deeper

- 4 -
Align
Forget Redesign

"Entrepreneurs (leadership) should always remember focusing on the best interest of the people they affect every day, whether that be their employees, shareholders or the community, will drive profits"
-- *Warren Buffett*

Conventional organizational change, directed by Management and Human Resources, typically involves training and development, as well as personal and team "motivation". These measures usually fails. Why? Are the people stupid? Can they not see the need for change? Do they not realize that if our organization cannot make these changes we will no longer be competitive? We will lose market share. There will be job cuts. We will eventually go out of business. Can they not see it?

Actually, they probably cannot. Or more precisely, your people look at things in a different way.

Bosses and organizations still tend to think that employees are paid to do a job and they should do what they're told. We are conditioned from an early age to believe that the way to teach and train, and to motivate people toward changing what they do, is to tell them, or persuade them. From our experiences at school we are conditioned to believe that skills, knowledge, and expectations are imposed on or 'put into' people by teachers, and later, by managers and bosses in the workplace.

But just because the boss says so, doesn't make it so. People today have a different perspective. And when you think about it, they're bound to. Imposing new skills and change on people doesn't work because:

- It assumes that people's personal aims, wishes, and needs are completely aligned with those of the organization, or that there is no need for such alignment.
- It assumes that people want, and can assimilate into their lives, given all their other priorities, the type of development or change that the organization deems appropriate for them.

Instead, organizations, managers, bosses, and business owners would do better to think first about exploring ways to align the aims of the business with the needs - total life needs - of their people. Most people who go to work are under no illusion that their main purpose in life is to do what their manager says, so that the organization can at the end of the year pay outrageously high rewards to greedy directors, and a big fat dividend to the shareholders. We (the workers) work so that others more gifted, fortunate, or aggressive, can profit from our efforts.

And god help you if you are running a management buyout company, intent on floating or selling out in the next two-to-five years, making the MBO equity-holders millionaires, leaving the employees, on whose backs these gains have been made, up the creek without a paddle, at the mercy of the new owners.

How on earth do you expect decent hardworking people to align with those aims? It's time for a radical re-think.

Fact one

People will never align with bad aims. Executive greed, exploitation, environmental damage, inequality, betrayal, and false promises are transparent to all decent folk. "Oh you want me to do this training, and adjust to your changes, so I can make more money for you and those who have ownership in this corporation? Sorry, no can do. I've got my own life to lead thanks very much."

And that's if you are lucky. Most staff will simply nod and smile demurely as if in servile acceptance. If they still wore caps they'd doff them.

And then nothing happens. Of course nothing happens. The people can't be bothered. Re-assess and re-align your organization's aims, beliefs, and integrity - all of it - with your people. Then they might begin to be interested in helping with new skills and change.

Fact two

People can't just drop everything and change, or learn new skills, just because you say so. Even if they want to change and learn new skills, they have a whole range of issues that keep them fully occupied for most of their waking hours - which were dumped on them by the organization in the first place.

"So you want me to attend this training course so that you can earn more. When I come back from two days away in some two star hotel, my pile of tasks to perform will just have magically disappeared, will it? And when I come to try to implement these new skills, and make all these new things happen, everyone will be completely instep, will they? Pull the other one. Again, no can do."

The reason why consulting with people is a rather good idea is that it saves you from yourself and your own wrong assumptions. Consulting with people does not mean that you hand over the organization to them - they wouldn't want the corporation anyway. No, consulting with people gives you and them a chance to understand the implications and feasibility of what you think needs to be done. And aside from this, consulting with people, and helping them to see things from both sides generally throws up some very good ideas for doing things better than you could have dreamt of by yourself. It helps you to see from both sides too.

Fact three

Organizations commonly say they don't have time to re-assess and re-align their aims and values, or don't have time to consult with people properly, because the organization is on the edge of a crisis.

Whose fault is that? Organizations get into crises because they ignore facts one and two. Ignoring these facts again will only deepen the crisis.

Crisis is no excuse for compromising integrity. Crisis is the best reason to re-align your aims and consult with people. Crisis demands leaders to wake-up and change the organization and its purpose - not change the people. When an organization is in crisis, the people are almost always fine - it'll be the organizational purpose and aims that stink.

So, whatever way you look at organizational change or redesign, you are kidding yourself if you think you can come up with a plan for change, then simply tell or persuade your people to implement it.

Instead, start by looking at your organization's aims and values and purposes:

What does your organization actually seek to do?
Whom does your organization benefit? And whom does it exploit?
Who are the winners, and who are the losers?
Does your organization have real integrity?
Are you proud of the consequences and implications of what your organization does?
And what do your people say to themselves about the way they relate to the organization?
Ask them!

"The role of a leader is to bring forth the genius and spirit of her people."

                                        --Sue Follon

Leadership as a process

Understanding leadership as a process requires us to think very differently about how we work with others. We will never mobilize leadership at the scale needed for significant progress on any complex issue without expanding our thinking about what leadership is, how it works, and how we can support it:

a. KNOWING oneself, the other team members, the company, and its purpose. Sharing information and understanding authentically with openness and humility lay the foundation for developing a shared sense of purpose out of which collective action grows. This involves connecting first with oneself to clarify one's intentions, values, beliefs, and worldview, then listening and asking questions that help individuals make meaning of their individual experience and understand each other better. Through this process groups begin to identify shared frustrations and aspirations.

b. TRUSTING in oneself, each other, and in company leadership.

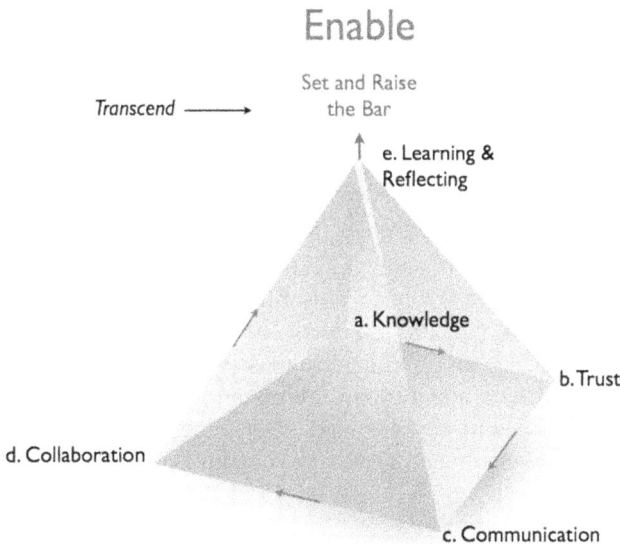

Enable

Transcend ⟶   Set and Raise
the Bar

↑ e. Learning &
Reflecting

a. Knowledge

b. Trust

d. Collaboration

c. Communication

Building relationships that foster trust and mutual understanding enables groups to work through conflicts and build a shared commitment and accountability. Most people are unaware how present and pervasive the impact of trust is in every relationship, in every organization, and in every interaction. When individuals take stock in the impact of trust relationships, it immediately affects their ability to increase their effectiveness. Whether it's high or low, trust is the hidden variable in the formula for organizational success. The traditional business formula says that strategy multiplied by execution equals results.

$$S \times E = R$$

But, we must include our hidden variable to this formula: trust – either the low-trust tax, which discounts the output, or the high-trust dividend, which multiplies it:

$$(S \times E) \times T = R$$

(Strategy x Execution) multiplied by Trust equals Results

c. COMMUNICATING in all directions –– upward, downward, and laterally. Communicating with superiors, direct reports, and colleagues is essential to building strong lines of communication. Part of establishing these lines of communication is utilizing tools to create communication structures that help the group set direction, plan, allocate resources, make decisions, engage the skills of individuals, and mobilize action.

d. COLLABORATING to produce a 'win-win' environment for the individual, team, company, and the customer. Part of this is uncovering shared concerns, frustrations, hopes, and goals across differences in culture and focus of work. As we recognize interdependence and find connections in our efforts, we uncover and unleash new opportunities to link and leverage our work. By finding common purpose and expanding our networks, we achieve new scale and create the conditions for transformative change.

e. LEARNING AND REFLECTING to clarify and evolve the collective purpose, more fully embody values, and renew mutual commitment. A continuous process that is integrated with action, it is the means we can use to hold ourselves collectively accountable for how we are doing, and for mobilizing to do better, individually and as a group. Reflection requires that individuals and groups understand themselves, inquire into the level of awareness, identities, and motives they bring to the workplace, and the personal work required to serve the collective purpose of the team, organization, community, or network.

A survey by the job-placement firm Manpower found 84 percent of employees intend to look around for a new job in 2011, up from 60 percent last year. CEOs of major U.S. companies "do not really put even 15% of their time into the people-development equation, and that's far less than needed' says Ram Charan (USA Today Dec. 2010)

Go
Deeper   www.effective-leadership.com/go-deeper

Keep the good ones

One of the most fundamental choices that employers make is whether to develop talent internally, by promoting from within the organization, or to hire talent from the outside. Large employers, in particular, have shifted their approach in recent years and now rely much more heavily on outside or lateral hiring. The prevalence of outside hiring can be seen in the exploding use of search firms and job boards, and in the growing rates of voluntary turnover in organizations - most people who quit do so for jobs elsewhere. The outside hiring trend contrasts sharply with the dominant model of previous generations: reorganizing firms by retraining and relocating existing employees into new roles.

The advantages to hiring employees from within the company are a greater company knowledge base, continuity, and an improved morale. An employee already in a business is likely to know more about the company's needs and will be able to approach a new position with the added perspective of his or her previous position. Hiring from within also brings continuity to a company. The talent of the individuals remains within the company, and is therefore re-invested. Finally, employees generally feel good about a company that promotes from within. It signals a company's belief in their people and in the quality of work that they do, and provides them with tangible evidence that their own efforts can bring about career advancement.

With that said, companies find gaps in their talent pipeline. The percent of companies in 2008 that identified this as their top challenge was actually up 16 percent over 2007, from 51 percent to 59 percent, respectively. As a matter of fact, surveys show 70 percent of companies indicate it is difficult to retain talent. Companies are seeing a tremendous increase in turnover, due partly to the fact that Generation X and Generation Y employees are more inclined to change jobs and careers in order to fulfill their personal needs and goals.

> Erma Bombeck once said that she would never go to a doctor whose office plants had died. Likewise, anyone should be wary of following a leader or serving in an organization that does not nourish and develop its entire people.

A deep understanding of what people truly respond to is vital to keeping them engaged. Each individual has his/her own wants and needs that have to be kept in the forefront of your mind as a leader.

People will respond when basic needs are being fulfilled: the need to be needed, the need for hope in a tough time, the need to feel in control, the need to blame something else for their troubles, the need to learn about something they don't know or are not supposed to know. As we move forward this principle underlies each movement in our journey.

- Part III -
The Ability to Keep Things Going

- 5 -
Imperative
Creating Profits and Growing the Business

"Execution is the chariot of genius."
-- William Blake

The repeatable day-to-day operating activities in a business are relatively clear-cut. Like blocking and tackling in football, they comprise the basic components of the daily activities of any organization – or any business – no matter the size. The authors' experience in private equity found most businesses, particularly small and middle market ones, tend to be activity focused doing the same things over and over. Being mainly activity-focused, without thinking about tomorrow will result in a lot of ups and downs, a potential capital shortage, and very likely, a decline in the value of the business.

In today's business world, corporations must be able to stay ahead of a rapid and constantly changing business environment effectively, and responsibly. They must be able to reduce the time it takes to discover new business challenges and align to them. Decisions must be made quickly and they must be done right the first time out. Corporations need to address these issues. However, the answer is not to waste time on ill-conceived strategic projects or to simply mimic what others have done hoping to achieve the same results – the worst kind of "Cargo Cult" behavior. Such action, even if supported by the leadership, rarely produces business results of value.

In order to be competitive, corporations must alter their efforts to focus on the few vital projects that can produce the desired business results for changing market dynamics and raise the bar on what can be accomplished. It's time to replace the traditional strategic planning process and corporate development function, if they exist at all, with a new encompassing outcome-driven discipline that involves an attuned senior team that focuses and takes action on the key business value drivers: growth, profitability, and corporate responsibility (sometimes referred to as the triple bottom line).

> Cost cutting will long remain a strategic priority for companies, yet any successes they may have will erode with time. Research shows that only 10 percent of cost reduction programs sustain their results three years on.

With all of the latest and greatest concepts, seminars, webinars, and How-To books vying for your attention, you would think that growing, and increasing profits and the value of your business was as complicated as building the space shuttle. The fact is, there are only three ways to expand business.

1. **Increase the number of customers** - attract more prospects
2. **Increase the frequency of purchase** - convert more prospects to customers
3. **Increase the number of units sold** - increase the average dollars per sale, and/or increase the frequency of purchases

In establishing how to grow your business, just ask: Is this going to increase the number of customers? The number of times my customers buy from me? The average value of each purchase my customers make from me?

A company may decide to accelerate its growth by:

Developing new business - develop areas, which may or may not be connected with its traditional business areas, by exploiting some competitive advantage that it may have. Once a company has decided to enter into a new business area(s), it has to explore various ways of achieving its aims. Basically, there can be three alternatives available to it: the formation of a new company, the acquisition of an existing company, or a merger with an existing company. Which of these options is to be accepted will depend on the company's assessment of various factors, including in particular, the cost that it is prepared to incur, the likelihood of success, and the degree of managerial control that it requires to retain. For a firm desiring immediate growth and quick returns, mergers can offer an attractive opportunity as they obviate the need to start from scratch and reduce the cost of entry into an existing business.

Almost 50% of businesses die within their first year of existence. After 5 years it's 80% who've died off. In 10 years it's 96%. 500,000 businesses are started every year. At the end of 10 years there are only 20,000 of them left. And these are the numbers from good times. See figure on Business Growth Cycle.

Go
Deeper   www.effective-leadership.com/go-deeper

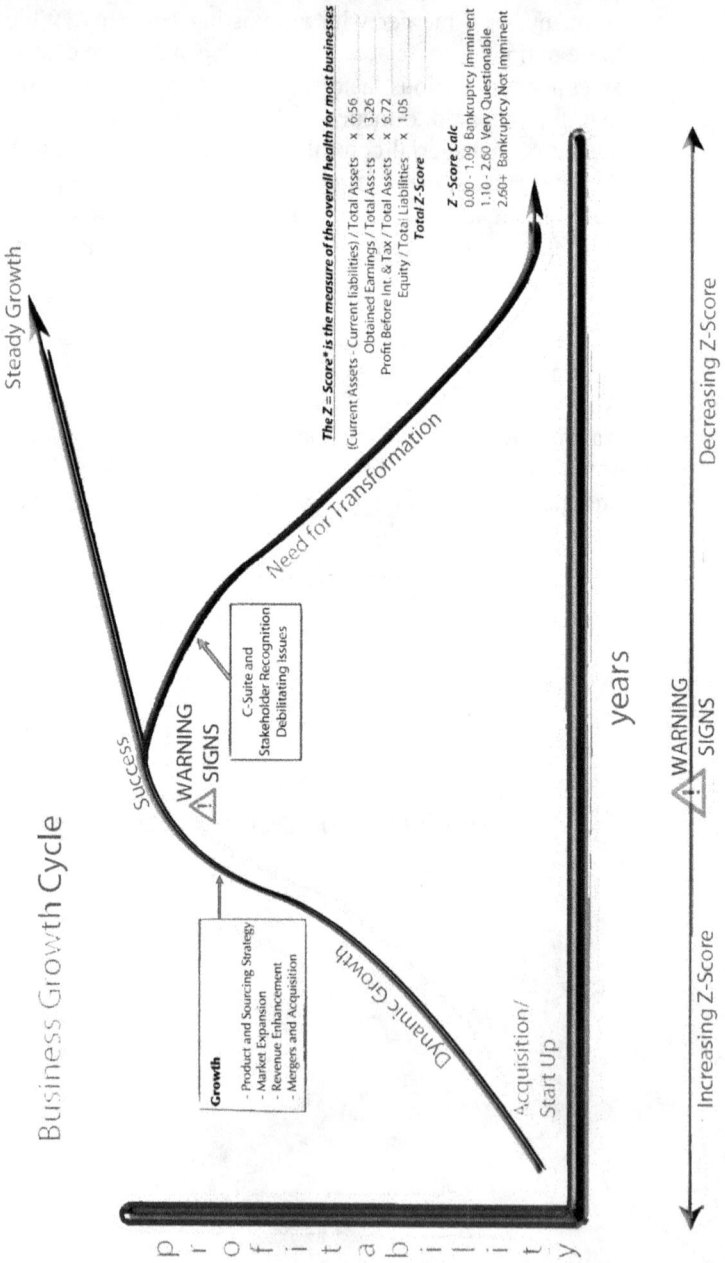

Business Growth Cycle

profitability — (y-axis)

years — (x-axis)

Acquisition/ Start Up

Dynamic Growth

Success

Steady Growth

Need for Transformation

Growth
- Product and Sourcing Strategy
- Market Expansion
- Revenue Enhancement
- Mergers and Acquisition

WARNING SIGNS
- C-Suite and Stakeholder Recognition
- Debilitating Issues

WARNING SIGNS

Increasing Z-Score — Decreasing Z-Score

The Z = Score* is the measure of the overall health for most businesses

(Current Assets - Current Liabilities) / Total Assets	x 6.56
Obtained Earnings / Total Assets	x 3.26
Profit Before Int & Tax / Total Assets	x 6.72
Equity / Total Liabilities	x 1.05
Total Z-Score	

Z - Score Calc
0.00 - 1.09 Bankruptcy Imminent
1.10 - 2.60 Very Questionable
2.60+ Bankruptcy Not Imminent

Business Model

In our experience, a business model (systems view) is the foundation - for examining, understanding, and describing just how a business operates to make a profit, as well as for addressing its future. In the author's tenure in private equity, he found that the business plans that were presented for a capital infusion were completely unprepared for investors. A business model template became the main tool for uncovering and fixing deficiencies in order to make an investment that worked to create the necessary margins to fuel growth. "Margin is oxygen for a business. Without adequate margin (profits), all functions in your business will be short of breath".

A business model is simply a working description that includes the general details about the operations of a business. The components that are contained within a business model will address all functions of the business, including expenses, revenues, operating strategies, corporate structure, and sales and marketing procedures. Generally speaking, anything that has to do with the day-to-day functionality of the corporation can be said to be part of the business model.

Kerr Pumps success story

The potential of successfully evolving a business over time through continuous evaluation and adjustment of eight business model components is dramatically illustrated by Kerr Pumps, a privately held mid-market company.

Kerr Pumps Corporation was founded in Ada, Oklahoma in 1946 to supply the thriving oil & gas industry with dependable, well-engineered, high performance pumps. In 1992, the facility was relocated to Sulphur, Oklahoma to enable growth and improve accessibility to major transportation arteries. In 1996, with new ownership at the helm, the product line was diversified to include models and options for a wide array of industrial applications. In 2008, a new complimentary product was developed and introduced that literally doubled its business.

Private Equity Firm - Business Model

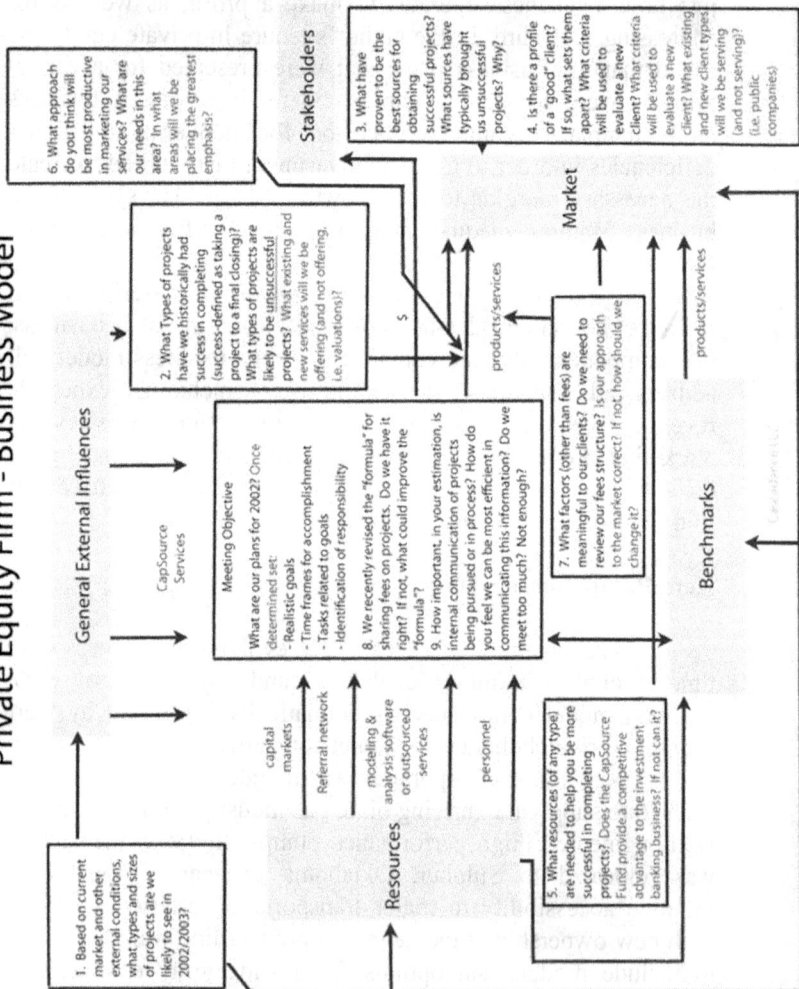

General External Influences

Stakeholders

Market

Benchmarks

Resources

CapSource Services

1. Based on current market and other external conditions, what types and sizes of projects are we likely to see in 2002/2003?

2. What Types of projects have we historically had success in completing (success-defined as taking a project to a final closing)? What types of projects are likely to be unsuccessful projects? What existing and new services will we be offering (and not offering, i.e. valuations)?

3. What have proven to be the best sources for obtaining successful projects? What sources have typically brought us unsuccessful projects? Why?

4. Is there a profile of a "good" client? If so, what criteria will be used to evaluate a new client? What criteria will we be used to evaluate a new client? What existing and new client types will we be serving (and not serving) (i.e. public companies)

5. What resources (of any type) are needed to help you be more successful in completing projects? Does the CapSource Fund provide a competitive advantage to the investment banking business? If not can it?

6. What approach do you think will be most productive in marketing our services? What are our needs in this area? In what areas will we be placing the greatest emphasis?

7. What factors (other than fees) are meaningful to our clients? Do we need to review our fees structure? Is our approach to the market correct? If not, how should we change it?

Meeting Objective

What are our plans for 2002? Once determined set:
- Realistic goals
- Time frames for accomplishment
- Tasks related to goals
- Identification of responsibility

8. We recently revised the "formula" for sharing fees on projects. Do we have it right? If not, what could improve the "formula"?

9. How important, in your estimation, is internal communication of projects being pursued or in process? How do you feel we can be most efficient in communicating this information? Do we meet too much? Not enough?

capital markets

Referral network

modeling & analysis software or outsourced services

personnel

products/services

products/services

Kerr Pumps is vastly expanding from year to year and "attribute[s] our success to our assurance of the dependability of our core products and most importantly, our loyal, dedicated group of people striving for excellence each and every day". Today Kerr is a formidable competitor in its industry segment and a frequent acquisition target by major corporations.

> Future success is 20% how we do things and 80% why we do things

Starting with the why is a reversal in the normal mindset of putting activity first: "start with purposes and principles before considering means," or, less abstractly, "start with the reasons why you're wanting to do something before moving to the hows, whats, and whens of the matter."

> The business case is the why and the action steps are the how - in that order!

A business case (why) is perspective, that is, the Future Picture and direction. A business case involves the big picture, the overall plan, and how those plans will achieve goals and objectives. It involves deciding who the important stakeholders are, and which of them will be the recipients (or the targets) of business activities.

A business case is the framework used to make decisions that will benefit the future outcome of the business. In other words, a business case is the set of directions, or map, you make to enhance the situation and position within the business' overall market.

Without a well thought out business case, the company is merely like a person wandering uselessly in the dark. There is neither a planned direction to go in the future, nor the methods to get there. Action steps and the business case are always relative to one another, and together they bridge the gap between ends and means.

To succeed in a business environment, it is vital to set a business case connected to activities. If you have a solid understanding of where you want to be at some defined point in the future, it becomes a relatively simple exercise to create a set of activities to get you there. If you know where you are going, there will be a way to get there – always.

Action steps (how) are specifically created and selected to reach particular and measurable objectives. Action steps are the actual ways in which business cases are executed. If not careful, selecting action steps that are not based on a business case may end up simply being quick fixes for the day-to-day operating activities that can bring short term gain, but will not lead to long-term success unless rigorously applied in the context of a business case. They must be part of an overall plan for success. Therefore, it is critical to ask of each selected action, what will it do to achieve the overall business case?

Recognize that there is a difference between the business case and action steps, and do not confuse the two. The company that clearly understands that difference is the company that will be the most successful, the most durable, and the most profitable.

"Look before you leap" is an old proverb, dating back to at least 570 B.C. Before proceeding with the carrying out of any opportunistic business case - check its potential against this simple formula: Value + Capability + Realization of Value that's greater than the Cost + Risk. Or, in short, $(V + Ca + RoV) > (Co + Ri)$. The three factors represented on the left hand side of the equation that must "add up" to be greater than those on the right:

Value
Any action(s) undertaken need to be based on reaching the value of the desired outcome.

Capability
Address the issue by determining what training, experience, confidence, and other needs there are to actualize the business case.

Realization of Value
Once you determine the above, the organization also needs to be able to provide the environment that will enable achievement. Again, the preceding three factors must be greater than the sum of the two factors on the right hand side of the equation that represent obstacles in the way of realizing the business case objectives. These factors are:

Cost

For any effort there is a cost in terms of time, effort, and/or resources. These costs can also change over time. By taking the time early on to understand the factors that need to be weighed when making a commitment decision, you will be in a stronger position to negotiate work distribution, prioritize tasks, and access resources.

Risk

There are different tolerances for what is believed risky. For some, making a minor mistake or working on a project that uses a technology out of their comfort zone may hold a level of risk. Consider what you can do to reduce the perceived risk. Perhaps you can break a complex project into phases to increase the other person's feeling of safety by limiting the scope of the activity. Other strategies include sharing the risk or formulating an exit option.

To get started estimates are good enough; rate each factor from 1 – 5. See figure – Business Model and Improvement Focus, from our client, an architectural roof manufacturer.

Business Model and Improvement Focus

Company Improvement Objective: Generate 8% EBITDA Annually

Performance Management	Growth Management	Cost Management
"Looking at the business on a weekly basis"	"Looking at ways we can grow the customer, revenue and profit"	"Looking for ways we can take cost out of the business"
◉Budget ◉Revenue Forecast	◉Demand Creation ◉Margin Management	◉Material Cost
Offerings Management	**End to End Process Management**	**Leadership Workforce Management**
"Looking for new revenue and margin"	"Looking for ways to simplify and improve processes"	"Looking for ways to make the people more effective"
◉Re-roofing ◉Composite Roofing	◉Office ◉Manufacturing	◉Leadership ◉Organization

In the new outcome-driven operating discipline alluded to earlier, the act of strategic planning and execution differs greatly from the staid traditional form, which often relied on formal, detailed programs and procedures written primarily for an annual report. The new discipline, referred to as *Enterprise Development Leadership*, which incorporates what others have termed shared, collaborative, complex, or distributed leadership, guides planning and execution as a process. Leadership functions are spread across multiple individuals and teams. The company's business model, financial priorities, and strategic imperatives are shared to align the organizational objectives. Rather than fixed plans created by a few senior executives, an organization develops open, flexible plans that are fully shared and embraced by all. Revision may be more important than vision. Flexible, open strategic directions supplant rigid, fixed plans. These plans are not merely top management visions and programs, but are fully embraced and shared by the people involved in making them happen. The leader or the top leadership team still steps in periodically to make key decisions that keep the firm aligned. They bound the chaos that may otherwise occur by providing guiding principles and the use of structures and processes to vet and select the many ideas that filter up. In short, top-level formal leaders are still responsible, but their role changes. Leaders now keep everyone focused on the corporate vision and provide an environment where people do the right things as standard operating procedure.

Use improvised implementation rather than executing plans based on the numbers. The Enterprise Development organization improvises change, encourages experimentation, rewards small wins, and institutionalizes success throughout the organization.

No longer does implementation consist of the note-by-note execution of a prescribed plan. Just as in jazz improvisation, where every performer is a composer, in the Enterprise Development organization, every member -- whether on the front line or the executive suite -- is a strategic partner. In Enterprise Development, individuals and teams act in creative and autonomous ways to interpret the strategic direction and realize plans. The actual nature of the change gradually reveals itself through the spontaneous and creative actions of people from all parts of the organization. They coordinate and collaborate with others in the organization also experimenting with change. Over time, successes and accomplishments are reinforced and entrenched, modifying the formal structures, rewards, procedures, and systems of the organization.

Enterprise Development relies on action learning. Rather than reevaluating change efforts only at once-a-year planning sessions, or waiting for the slow learning that derives from experience or the traumatic learning that occurs from crisis. The action learning organization takes action, reflects, and adjusts course as it goes, seeking to enhance the speed and effectiveness by which it learns how to change.

Learning is not something that happens on its own. It is made to happen. Learning begins when those involved in an activity stop and examine how things are done. In Enterprise Development organizations, attempts are made to provide frequent, ongoing opportunities for such action-based learning. Enterprise Development organizations do not wait for problems to emerge or for crises to arise that compel reevaluation. Reflection becomes part of "the way we do things around here" and is built into the implementation of strategic change. Through this process, they question the original assumptions and search for deep, system (double-loop) solutions to problems.

Make no mistake, Enterprise Development requires new leadership practices--a shift that, in the words of CISCO CEO Jon Chambers, you could almost call "as revolutionary as the assembly line." At Cisco, among other things done to encourage collaboration, cross-functional boards and councils were created to quickly make strategic decisions and respond to new opportunities. Some larger organizations, in order to involve more in the process, have electronic feedback and voting. Some have open forums for discussion. Still others have committees that choose which ideas actually move forward. Collaboration as a way of operating is built into structures, reward systems, and HR practices. Consequently, leadership entails a new balance between networks and individuals, worldviews, practices, and freedom and control.

Execute

Transcend ———▸ Create Exceptional Value
& Meaning

e. Evaluate

f. adjust

a. Assess

b. Design

d. Monitor

c. Implement

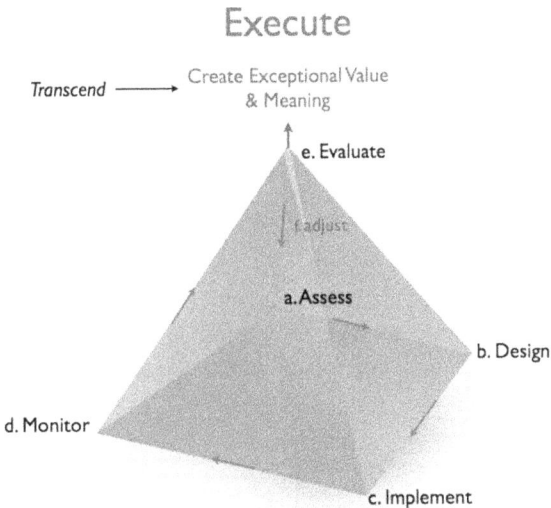

The Leading Pyramid aka The Enterprise Development Operating System (EDOS) involves a framework of six parts. These parts are common to all actions, although the details of how they are applied will depend on the characteristics of the objectives and the creativity of the participants:

a. Assess:
- Once you have decided on your business case, define measurable objectives and indicators.
- Explore the effects of alternative strategies.
- Document predicted outcomes.
- Identify key uncertainties and assumptions.
- Document the basis for decisions.

b. Design:
- Design a plan(s) to test key assumptions/resolve key uncertainties (apply the principles of experimental design to design of actions).
- Define details of monitoring plan.

c. Implement:
- Follow the plan.
- Document deviations from the plan.

d. Monitor:
- Monitor implementation and effectiveness, according to the plan.

e. Evaluate:
- Compare actual outcomes to predicted outcomes.
- Assess which assumption is supported by data.
- Document and communicate results.

f. Adjust:
- Close the loop!
- Revise assumptions as necessary.
- Update models (mental models and computer models).
- Confirm or adjust actions/strategies.
- Identify further uncertainties that should be resolved.

Used wisely, an EDOS can help address some of the challenges presented in traditional strategic planning execution, but it is not a panacea. It can resolve disagreements over how to reach a desired future condition, but it cannot resolve disagreements over values or what the desired future condition should be. EDOS is like a compass: once your destination is defined, it can help you find your way there, even when the pathway is obscured by uncertainty and complexity.

An aligned and integrated organization that utilizes an EDOS is the optimal state in which the organization, customers, and key processes work in concert to propel growth and profits. When business leaders implement the kind of alignment shown, the whole organization enjoys greater customer satisfaction, greater employee satisfaction, and greater returns for stakeholders and investors. To do this, you de-emphasize hierarchy and distribute authority, information, knowledge, and customer data. As a result, every employee, top to bottom, understands the strategy and goals of the business. Consequently, everyone knows how his/her work contributes to it.

There are many ways to measure alignment, but it can only be achieved through Enterprise Development Leadership. Implementing such strategies develops leadership in each unit of your operation and at different levels of your organization. You actually end up engaging employees, and enabling and empowering them to act and know what must be done.

With this kind of clear vision and strong communication, you can allow your organization to run with tasks and projects independent of your day-to day management, freeing you for higher level leadership tasks and responsibilities.

Go
Deeper   www.effective-leadership.com/go-deeper

Focus on performance over time. The ultimate concern of Enterprise Development is to quantitatively improve performance (sustainability) over time. This can apply to the enterprise as a whole, or to a key function of interest e.g. sales. This means answering some challenging questions:

- Why is performance following its current path?
- Where will performance go if we continue along the same path?
- How can we design a robust strategy to radically improve that performance in the future?

This exhibit shows how these questions looked for Starbucks after the difficulties it experienced in 2007/8.

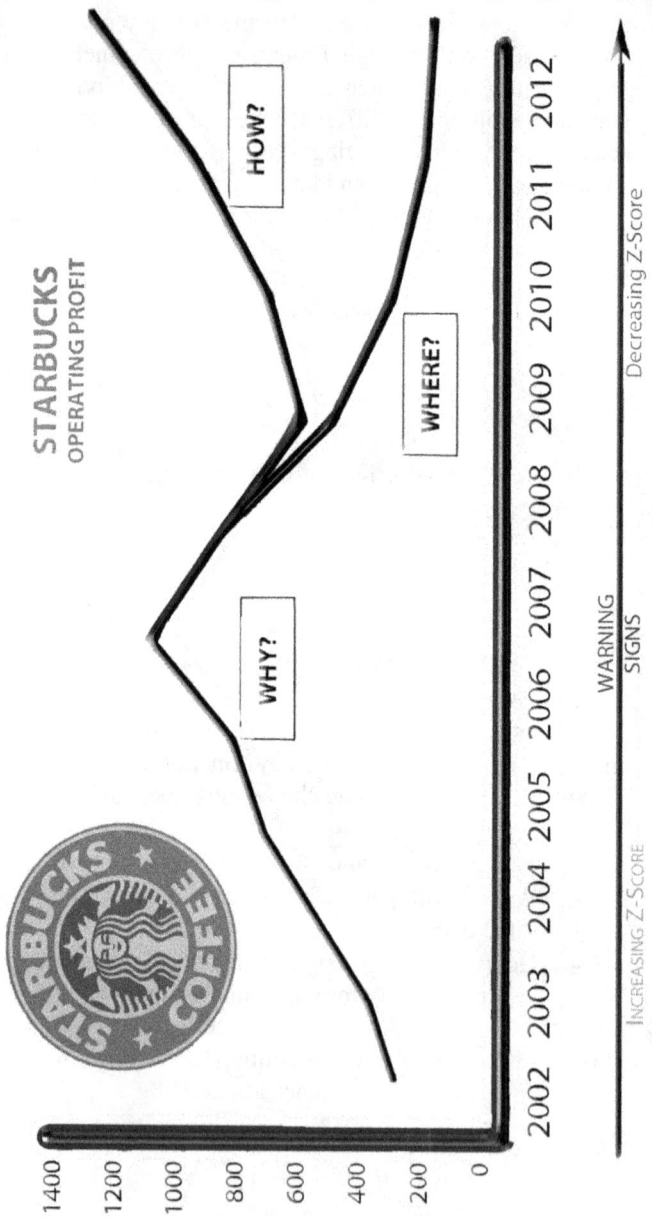

STARBUCKS
OPERATING PROFIT

HOW?

WHERE?

WHY?

2002 2003 2004 2005 2006 2007 2008 2009 2010 2011 2012

0 200 400 600 800 1000 1200 1400

INCREASING Z-SCORE

WARNING SIGNS

Decreasing Z-Score

In 2008, the economy had stalled and consumers were balking at spending $4 per drink, even at a familiar place. Howard Schultz announced that the company had "lost its way," becoming too standard and corporate and less entrepreneurial, less like a local coffee shop. The chain then closed stores on a broad scale for the first time. Would Starbucks even be around in 3 years, or would it take its place among the dearly departed, driven out by a tough economy?

Fast-forward a year later. Starbucks blows its Q4 numbers out of the water – sales were up 4% driven by both increases in store traffic and average ticket price. If that wasn't enough, the company's margins were up by 8.5% to 13%. Starbucks returned to its growth mode and launched 100 new locations in the U.S., and another 200 worldwide.

How was it done? Clean execution, new products, and a motivated sales force all contributed in a big way to the company's transformative success. Starbucks now uses an enterprise development approach to engage employees in surveying customers for ideas, making suggestions for improvement, identifying logistical issues, and, when an idea is selected for development and launch (which they actually are!), providing timetables and commentary on the launch. Imagine that! A company that asks customers for ideas, permits them to prioritize the ideas, and actually assigned relatively senior people to engage in conversation with their customer community!

- 6 -
Meaning
Commitment to a Wider Impact

"When you've finished getting yourself ready in the morning, you must go get the planet ready."
                                                    -- The Little Prince

Our book was inspired by an awareness of, and concern for, the challenges and complexities faced by business leaders in the twenty-first century. The shift from the industrial to the post-industrial era has brought about a new and complex network of activities globally. The increasing uncertainties and divides facing the business world - as well as society in general - have led to the realization that the old paradigms and leadership approaches are no longer effective. The shift to a networked society demands a shift in the consciousness levels, the virtues, and the values of business leaders and their boards.

> "The purpose of leadership isn't to increase shareholder value or the productivity of work teams, though effective leadership does these things. Rather, the purpose of leadership is to change the world around you in the name of your values, so you can live those values more fully and use them to make life better for others."
> *McKinsey Quarterly Oct 2010*

This view predicates the premise that, under certain conditions and in certain situations, business is an important driver of transformation in general. Business has the ability and the power to influence the whole of which it is a part, such as societies, communities, and environments. The assumption that business is an important catalyst of change in society and its leaders are accountable for the creation of a sustainable and meaningful environment defines its role of service toward the whole. In other words, businesses accept some responsibility for all or most processes in which they may be involved. Business leaders' values and worldviews directly influence their decision-making processes.

In Chapter 1 we reflected upon the nature of the human person with his/her remarkable innate ability to know, reflect, conceive and create new ideas. We saw how the human being is capable of transcending the world around them, stepping back, and reaching beyond the here and now. All of this points to the spiritual nature found in every person. Each, with their human faculties of intellect and will, is capable of going beyond themselves. Taken a step further, a new consciousness or values-based approach to business and society, i.e. spirituality, incorporates the leader's values and worldview dimensions into making transformation and sustainability a reality. The spirituality needed provides a holistic, values-based approach and, consequently, the capacity to deal with complexity and change not present in previous management frameworks. Quantum physics, or the "new science", as initiated by physicists such as Heisenberg and Bohm helps us to understand, from a slightly different perspective, the approach we illustrate here. Scientists, striving to observe the sub-nuclear world found that their very act of doing so changed the system they were observing. Heisenberg' uncertainty principle opened the door to the deep world of probabilistic mathematics as a way of observing things around us. The same holds true of the "new science" as it related to observing objects at very large distances (stars, galaxies – aka cosmology). In both the cases (studying the very small and very large,) the human intellect is challenged as never before, and the distinction between science and philosophy is blurred. Today, with modern String and Unified Field Theory, scientists, like never before, bring together science and philosophy in order to understand the world around them. Here we do the same, looking to understand business from a broader perspective, one that sees leadership and its development more collectively, taking into account the spiritual abilities. Our previous book, *Outcome Management*, when describing leadership and spirituality, explained that "those who lead with vigor, stamina of spirit, and courage, often raise not only the quality of their own performance, but also the performance of those who look to them." We must also recognize three other authors, Robert Terry, Jim Collins, and Richard Barrett, who juxtapose the principles of spirituality and spiritual intelligence with leadership. These three authors, respectively and collectively, argue in favor of the involvement of a new holistic consciousness and an authenticity in servant leadership. They assume that these leadership qualities enhance interdependency and may lead to sustainability. We agree that spirituality and business leadership enable a process of transformation in people, organizations, and society, as well as being possible catalysts for creating meaning, fulfillment, and sustainability. This book makes the argument that people, as an integral part of the world, are being challenged to change not only themselves, but by virtue of a sharpened intelligence and consciousness, also the world (organization) in which they behave, through their leadership conduct. This requires leaders to better understand and interpret a new world, and to reflect on themselves and their organization from more dimensions than the purely profit-based motive.

The triple bottom line was first fully explained by John Elkington in his 1997 book, *Cannibals With Forks: The Triple Bottom Line of 21st Century Business*. The triple bottom line, a measure of an organization's profits but also its impact on people and the planet, expresses a company's sustainability on both a local and global scale.

Herman Miller, a renowned furniture company, committed to including as many expressions of human aptitude and potential as possible in its community of customers, suppliers, contractors, and employees through its inclusiveness and diversity initiative. Herman Miller believes that changing demographics, technology, and business conditions have clearly demonstrated the critical importance of inclusiveness to the company's success. The company, a globally recognized industry leader in environmentally responsible product design and manufacturing, has day-to-day operations that reflect a triple bottom line of financial, environmental, and social equity.

Wider Impact

As the corporate world begins to come to grips with what sustainability means to their companies and to their survival, more and more companies are embracing values related to sustainability and are defining actions to support them. However, varying definitions of 'sustainability' abound; some are merely looking for ways to comply with new regulations, while others are looking for better ways to manage their electrical and water resources, and reduce their carbon footprint. Still others are taking much broader approaches and looking at how the company does business with its shareholders, suppliers, customers, and employees. No matter how narrow or broad a company defines its efforts, success will require activities that enable change within the company.

The popular notion that corporations have a responsibility to give back to the public—and that doing so will make a company more profitable—is a flawed strategy at best, and at worst, a dangerous one, writes Aneel Karnani, an associate professor at the University of Michigan's business school, in an opinion piece in *The Wall Street Journal*. He and others argue that Corporate Social Responsibility (CSR) is a weak, misguided and ineffective concept simply because companies' primary purpose is to make money. Unless an organization's socially responsible efforts are a genuine attempt to create more profit (for example, Toyota pushing the market towards more efficient cars) they will be of little value to anyone.

According to this argument, the suggestion that companies should focus on more than just profit and care about the community and the environment, implies that these extra things don't generate profit, which means they'll be the first ideas dropped when the going gets tough. If this argument holds true, we have our work cut out for us.

The terms CSR and Sustainability are interrelated and many use them interchangeably as well. However, we find it useful to distinguish between CSR and Sustainability in a business context.

For business, it is useful to think about CSR in the context of the vision/mission of the business. What are the responsibilities of the business, why does it exist, and how it will go about meeting those responsibilities and goals.

It is useful to think about Sustainability in the context of how the business will operate; especially with a focus on the natural resources it consumes both directly (e.g., coal) and indirectly (e.g., electricity). How will the business be operated in way that allows it to make a profit today while not compromising the ability of future generation to meet their own needs.

Business' first responsibility to society is to operate at a profit and only slightly less important is the necessity for growth. Business is the wealth creating and wealth-producing organ of our society. Business must maintain its wealth producing resources intact by making adequate profits to offset the risks of economic activity. And it must increase the wealth creating and wealth producing capacity of these resources with them the wealth of society. Many years ago, the author's MBA economics professor made a strong point that "the main purpose of business was not to make profits; instead it was to produce goods and services with profits being a by-product." Market failure occurs when the cost of a good or service is higher than the price that individuals are able or willing to pay; yet the social benefits from that goods or services makes availability worthwhile for maintaining a healthy, productive society. We define social responsibility as the practice of responding to market failures with transformative, financially sustainable innovations aimed at solving social problems. Most importantly, business must realize that it must consider the impact of every business policy and business action upon society. It has to consider whether the action is likely to promote the public good, to advance the basic beliefs of our society, or contribute to its stability, strength and harmony.

Creating positive social impact is no longer reserved for non-profits and charitable organizations. Over the past decade, businesses have begun to assume a larger role in their local, national and global communities. The double, or even triple, bottom line of economic, social, and environmental return for shareholders and stakeholders is slowly changing the way business is done. Research has demonstrated that employees are more motivated and productive when they find meaning through their work. Additionally, many companies are seeing corporate social responsibility not as a separate part of their business but as a crucial activity in understanding and addressing social issues that could have long-term implications for their own viability.

Often, those enabling transformation to support organizational initiatives use models of change management. These models, however, prove inadequate for change enablement needed to support sustainability efforts, broad and narrow, because they differ substantially from the change management of other corporate initiatives. Sustainability initiatives are far more complex than almost any other corporate initiative that we have observed or assisted with in our years of consulting. Thus, traditional models for change are unlikely to be sufficient.

Certainly some parts of traditional models will apply. However, we do believe that, fundamentally, our approach to enablement for sustainability requires a new paradigm:

1. The changes required to enable successful sustainability efforts are enormously transformational.
2. The far-reaching implications of the 'triple bottom line' continue to evolve with more data, advances in technologies, et cetera. Thus, the change process must be organic.
3. Initiatives usually include a very broad range of stakeholders who must work together across internal and external boundaries to accomplish change.
4. Sustainability generally energizes the workforce. Resistance is more likely to occur at the top of the hierarchy than at the bottom.

For a solution, we have returned to our pyramid metaphor. The first and most famous pyramids are located at Giza in Cairo, Egypt. Many different civilizations built pyramids, yet they were from all over the world, from China to South America. In an age when transcontinental communication was impossible, what drove our ancestors to build such similar structures?

The answer is physics. The laws of physics affect the building of tall structures equally for all civilizations in every part of the world. The pyramid distributes weight really well, making it the most stable structure. Its wide base prevents the building from toppling or sinking into the ground. In all civilizations, engineers analyzed the same givens and variables and came to the same conclusions. It really is that simple.

<u>Complexity is simplicity repeated</u>

Today, effective leadership is everyone's business, from the boardroom to the mailroom. No longer can one person know or do it all. We depend on each other to produce mutually satisfying outcomes. Using fractals to illustrate, this discourse proposes the concept of distributed—or shared—leadership that is self-similar at every scale. Simple principles of effective leadership can be replicated at all levels of an organization, which in this case refers to all entities involved whether a group of individuals, or a corporation who get together for a common purpose.

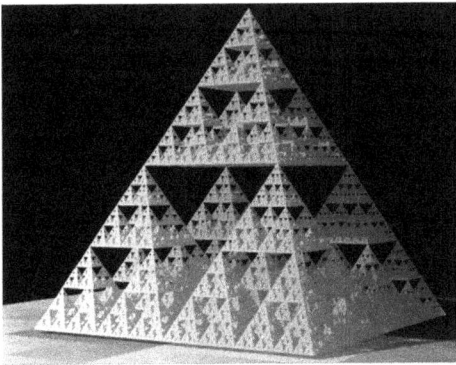

Almost universally, pyramid structure imagery is used to represent corporate, governmental, and military organizational hierarchies. The hierarchical organization depicted as a fractal has groups of small pyramid structures within a larger pyramid structure. Each fractal is as *a company within a company* similar to the company as the whole. The pattern remains the same no matter how many times it is multiplied. To have a leadership structure that grows with the body, we need to have a similar **design** that maintains its own integrity no matter how many times it is multiplied. This can provide a pattern and direction for units exploding in a chain reaction, something the traditional hierarchical organizational model cannot. The degree to which a company is centralized and formalized, the number of levels in the company hierarchy, and the type of departmentalization the company uses are key elements of a company's structure. These elements of structure affect the degree to which the company is effective and innovative as well as employee attitudes and behaviors at work. These elements come together to create mechanistic and organic structures. Mechanistic structures are rigid and bureaucratic and help companies achieve efficiency, while organic structures are decentralized, flexible, and aid companies in achieving innovativeness and deal with challenges such social impact issues. Although organic organization structures can be comparatively more complicated and difficult to form the benefits are worth the effort – with an understanding of fractals the task can be greatly simplified.

From – Mechanistic	To - Organic
Function driven	Purpose driven
Closed	Open
Parts	Whole
Top down–hierarchical	Local focus
Controlled	Empowered
Corporate	Boundaryless[1]
Centralized	Distributed/Networked
Departmentalized	Connected
Sameness	Diversity
Stability	Growth/Change

(1)"Boundaryless" references removal of artificial barriers such as organizational levels, functional department, or firm boundaries that could impact delivery of value to the customer. One of the best early examples of this was when all quality control functions were delegated to the production units; the quality department was turned into quality assurance as a service provider overseeing the Quality Management System thus making the whole process more effective and efficient.

Walk into any bookstore, look at the books on the shelves, and you'll see very few that address the actual organizational structure of a business. Most writing about business doesn't actually address the structure of the organization. There are ideas about marketing and sales, about human resources management, product innovation, and leadership, but not really that much about the structure of the organization itself. If you find something about structure, the focus is primarily on measuring performance i.e. balanced scorecards. And as valuable as measurement tools are to performance enhancement, by themselves they tend to result in incremental improvement at best.

The chief problem affecting organizational performance today is not the ability of people to perform, but the structure within which they do so. This is unfortunate because the design of the organization determines whether your purpose has a possibility of being fulfilled or whether your people will have the opportunity to fulfill their potential service to the business.

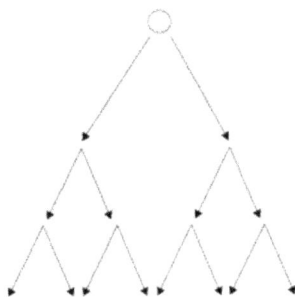

Hierarchy (tree structure)   Network (intelligent structure)

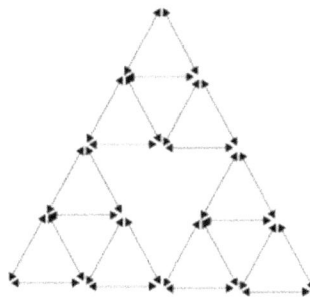

In traditional hierarchical structures, leadership is a function of position, authority, and power. In collaborative structures, leadership is a function of the character and influence of people in a social context. Personal character, communication skills, and the ability to share power are keys.

While this may seem rather mundane and ordinary for many of us, it is revolutionary in the context of hierarchy. This is so because it means that leadership is not held as a private privilege, but rather shared as a common responsibility. It is this way of work that is creeping into the hierarchies of organization as changing them from within.

The bureaucratic structure that constrains many large, complex organizations requires dramatic levels of change in order to function well; thus the rise of social connection as the organizing principle of "impact" organizations in the future.

The pathway to this approach is in appreciating the importance of the relationship dimension to the creation of strength and impact in an organization. From that perspective barriers to interaction and collaboration lower or are removed, enabling people to become more engaged with the purpose and mission of the organization, and to do so in relationship with other members of their organizational community.

Organizations are not just policies, processes, and operating structures. They are places where people interact for the purpose of achieving the goals of the company.

The problem with most organizations is that they are not organized around people, but around the processes that constitute the organization's operating system. The effect of this problem is that it creates, not a culture of collaboration, but one of compliance to the processes that are designed into the system. This is why people in these systems are often referred to as cogs in a machine.

The solution to this problem is not dramatic or radical. It is, however, a shift of perspective from a process orientation to a people one.

The key take away is that many kinds of organizational structures exist. All kinds of organizational structures, including hierarchical, linear, and matrix, can accomplish their goals efficiently when appropriate knowledge organizes the parts and connects them to the whole. Therefore, the future organizational chart may look as it does today, but more organic in nature; the protocols will be more open, communication will be freer, employees will act empowered, and each box on the chart will be operating independently, with authority and power of its own for the good of the entire organization.

> Can we rely on governments to achieve a sustainable world?
> *"Like it or not, the responsibility for insuring a sustainable world falls largely on the shoulders of the world's enterprises, the economic engines of the future."*
> Professor, Stewart Hart Kenan-Flager Business School, USA

Every business has to realize that it is a "co-creative eco-system" that includes its employees, partners, competitors and customers and the way they are motivated to create and realize value is the only measure of success. An example of creating an effective and collaborative eco-system business is when companies use a technology platform to advance their operations. For example, **social media** networks reach thousands of individuals through websites, text messaging accounts, and other interactive items for both work and enjoyment. Companies of all types can work with social media companies to leverage the technology in these websites into a corporate-based structure. Additionally, companies may use the social media network to reach new and current consumers with product offerings. The collaboration results in new profit potential and social impact opportunities for companies. Social media tools help with the functionality of these more organic organizations, still most people need time together to make their work experience more complete and to be afforded the opportunity to be involved in projects with social impact. To this end, we encourage in-person meetings for the whole company at least every 6 months. These meetings usually last one week and we suggest they be held as an organized retreat. Given the intensity of everyday work, there's a lot of pent-up excitement by the time of the retreat and the week tends to fly by. Attendees prepare in advance by thinking up potential projects that can be built and launched in a week. This turns the meetings into a kind of "hack week" with 2-3 person teams working on projects and commissioning and launching them at the end of the week (milestone group reviews need to be within 90 days). Time is also set aside for socializing, having fun excursions (hiking, sports games, etc.), and doing 10-minute lightning talks followed by Q&A (short talks by anyone in the company on whatever topic they feel like sharing).

Always keep in mind: all good leaders serve the interests of others, not just people who report to them and those they report to, but all stakeholders. Exceptional leaders model leadership for others. This is an indispensible tool for the success of individuals, teams, and organizations in the 21st century.

1. Leadership functions can be spread across multiple individuals and teams — even to those outside the firm
2. Leadership can be taken on by those not in formal leadership roles — in one of our client's organization almost 60% of employees self-identified as leaders
3. Change can be driven from the bottom up. At Southwest Airlines, for instance, front-line employees took the lead in devising new ways to reduce turnaround times and develop electronic ticketing.

Go
Deeper

www.effective-leadership.com/go-deeper

Business Models Beyond Profit

A business model for enduring social impact applies the same strategic rigor and financial savvy to social problem solving. It defines a course of action — generally spanning three to five years — that will guide your organization in generating another kind of profit: lasting social impact

Today, pressing issues are increasingly being solved through innovative business models. Before the tools, come the stories – identifying, analyzing, and profiling businesses, which hold significance far beyond the traditional business world. This significance might be social, environmental, and/or developmental impact. Many different terms are used for these types of businesses and ventures, such as: social business, social entrepreneurship, triple-bottom-line businesses, etc. Since we are particularly interested in the business models of these enterprises, we will use a working terminology and regroup these various definitions under the umbrella of "Business Models with an Impact". The real power of this trend, and a refined terminology, will surface when we push the project forward together as a group, when we share our knowledge and experience. The journey begins with you. What will you share?

What excites you about the potential of business models with an impact and social entrepreneurship?

Link to an image that represents the potential of business models beyond profit for you: Just put a URL in here.

If you were writing a book on business models with an impact, what would you put in it? Try to put in chapter titles.

What does "impact" mean to you? e.g. Social, Environmental, Developmental, Health…

What would you want to get out of a toolkit for business models with an impact? A toolkit is one of the goals of the project.

What do you want to contribute to this discussion? Again, a simple list of words will do.

What are three skills you can offer to the open process of business models beyond profit? Put a comma between your skills.

What are the coolest business models with an impact out there? i.e. social, environmental, or developmental impact

What are the challenges faced in creating a business model and social entrepreneurship venture that aims at having an impact? A simple list of words will do!

Is there a limit to how much money business models beyond profit and social entrepreneurship ventures should make compared to other businesses? Rank your thoughts:

	1	2	3	4	5	6	7	
No profit at all	☐	☐	☐	☐	☐	☐	☐	More prosperous than other businesses

How deeply are businesses integrating social and environmental impact into their organizations today? Rank your thoughts:

	1	2	3	4	5	6	7	
No business is having a positive impact	☐	☐	☐	☐	☐	☐	☐	Every business is conscious of its impact

How deeply might "impact" be integrated into businesses of the future? Rank your thoughts:

	1	2	3	4	5	6	7	
Business and impact can't be integrated	☐	☐	☐	☐	☐	☐	☐	All businesses can have a positive impact beyond profit

When did you first hear about the concept business with impact? Or social entrepreneurship, triple-bottom-line, and similar concepts?

	1	2	3	4	5	6	7	
Last week	☐	☐	☐	☐	☐	☐	☐	Decades ago

Who else should be involved in this project? Can you give us their contact? You can put a URL, name, company, organization, etc.

Go
Deeper

www.effective-leadership.com/go-deeper

- 7 -
Ascending
Incorporating Inspiration and Reflection

"The only permanent happiness is the pursuit of knowledge and the joy of understanding."
-- Walter Russell

Peter Drucker in *The Effective Leadership* (1966) argues that every person in a modern organization is an executive if, by virtue of his position or knowledge, he is responsible for a contribution that materially affects the capacity of the organization to perform and to obtain results. According to him, the largest working group will become what he calls knowledge workers.

Within each person is the often-untapped potential for enthusiasm and motivation that produces high job performance. Releasing this potential and energy in employees and peers is fundamental to achieving high performance in an organization. In most cases, all other things being equal, the difference between success and failure often lies in how well the organization can create an environment in which people are willing to expend the necessary energy and effort to ensure success. The defining characteristic of these knowledge workers is their education. Thus, development is more about providing the right goals, the right inspiration, the right tools, and clearly articulating how success or failure will be measured.

Perhaps the greatest lesson from Japanese auto manufacturers is that all employees are ultimately knowledge workers and that the role of the firm is to both encourage and support problem-solving by all employees. The companies recognize that front line assembly workers on the factory floor are in fact essential to performance improvement for the broader firm - the antithesis of a conventional view of knowledge workers. In encouraging and supporting problem solving by these employees, the Japanese automakers are able to give their work new meaning and unleash much more passion on the factory floor. The lesson is clear: we undermine our potential for performance improvement with labels that draw artificial boundaries through our workforce.

A values-based knowledge organization is less about setting rules for employees to follow, and more about working with them in establishing strategy, setting goals and measuring results.

If institutions and, indeed, nations are going to mobilize their entire workforce -- a desirable goal considering the increasing returns that characterize collaboration curves — we need to abandon this artificial distinction and look to redefine even jobs that appear highly routine to embrace and extend their creative aspects. We will begin to redefine all jobs, especially those performed at the front line (or, in an image that reveals our prevalent management mindset, the bottom of the Institutional

Pyramid), in ways that facilitate problem solving, experimentation, and tinkering. This will foster more widespread performance improvement. Everyone, even the most unskilled worker, will be viewed as a critical problem-solver and knowledge worker contributing to performance improvement.

The role of the knowledge organization was clearly highlighted at Time Warner Cable, which spun out of Time Warner in 2000 to create a company offering television, broadband Internet, and telephone services. It is now the second-largest cable company in the US, with 14 million subscribers.

When Time Warner talks about leaders, it does not mean just the top executives in the company. "We see everyone in our organization as a leader"

"Everything we say and do at every level has an impact on our customers, internal and external, so we need knowledgeable leaders and skilled employees supporting our mission and practicing our values."

Developing the right skillset for Time Warner Cable means focusing on talent development at all levels of the business, given that over 60% of its workforce has direct interaction with customers.

"Executive education is clearly a priority, as well as focusing on developing customer-facing employees within the organization, whether they are our installers, our techs visiting customers' homes, or agents in our call centers, We have so much focus on customer services. We know these are our heroes.

"Developing talent is a focused and interactive process, underlying that process are the values and mission of the organization. We use our leaders to teach whenever we can. For the development of leaders, there are no better learning opportunities than teaching others in the organization." Pat Crull, vice-president and chief learning officer for Time Warner Cable. *From CEO Online Magazine December 8, 2009.*

The new world of the 21st century is becoming more knowledge intensive, global, fast-paced, dynamic, and organic. Organizations operate constantly in flux, with the rapid pace of technological innovations, globalization, financial shifts, re-engineering, mergers and acquisitions. Organizations try to change, adapt, and become self-organized dynamic systems focusing on strategies of empowerment to enable and increase employee involvement and participation. The 21st century organization is about embracing members as whole persons, acknowledging not only their cognitive faculties but also their social, emotional, physical, and spiritual faculties, to engage their hearts and spirits as well as their minds. To do this an organization must be dedicated and passionate about making a positive difference in the lives of people, which can only grow from authentic enthusiasm, love, and concern.

Success in engaging our knowledgeable people and one of the most challenging tasks of leadership is turning intellectual knowledge into habitual behavior. The problem with lectures and seminars is that they usually teach us things we assume we are already doing. As Samuel Johnson wryly said, "common sense is the only thing in oversupply since we all assume we have more than we need."

Some examples, methods, and practices to incorporate inspiration and reflection in organizations include the following: reflective writing exercises, dialog journals using problem-posing questions, discussion circles, support groups, dialog spaces in workshops, book discussion groups, spiritual reflections on change, management development retreats, interactive art projects, interactive theater or role-plays, games and plays, storytelling, breathing and relaxation exercises, diversity framing, team-building, trust-building activities, meditation, moments of silence, and self awareness tests and exercises that focus on understanding one's identity and values systems.

New knowledge is available to everyone. But many people refuse to see, to hear, or realize because this conflicts with their paradigms, with their innate conceptions of reality. "There are none so blind as those who will not see". The Internet is a useful source of knowledge, but at the same time can be used by people only to reinforce their belief systems rather than add new knowledge; when there is information that is not a match they turn on their conceptual filters.

A new book written by Nicholas Carr titled *The Shallows: How the Internet is Changing the Way We Think, Read and Remember* suggests that the amount of time we spend on the Internet is changing the very structure of our brains – damaging our ability to think and to learn. Carr writes, "by dramatically reducing the cost of creating, storing, and sharing information, computer networks have placed far more information within our reach than we ever had access to before. And the powerful tools for discovering, filtering, and distributing information developed by companies like Google ensure that we are forever inundated by information of immediate interest to us--and in quantities well beyond what our brains can handle...Information overload has become a permanent affliction, and our attempts to cure it just make it worse. The only way to cope is to increase our scanning and our skimming, and to rely even more heavily on the wonderfully responsive machines that are the source of the problem."

Anderson and Rainie look at the positive side. "The social benefits of Internet use will far outweigh the negative. Over the next decade, according to experts who responded to a survey about the future of the Internet. They say this is because email, social networks, and other online tools offer 'low☐friction' opportunities to create, enhance, and rediscover social ties that make a difference in people's lives. The Internet lowers traditional communications constraints of cost, geography, and time; and it supports the type of open information sharing that brings people together." *Janna Quitney Anderson, Elon University; Lee Rainie, Pew Research Center's Internet & American Life Project.*

A Case Study
International Oil and Gas
Exploration and Production Company

A division of a very large international E & P Company is currently focusing efforts on under-producing oil and gas fields worldwide. The division brings new technology, management systems, organizational structure, leadership and technical training to bear on new ventures. Their latest and most challenging project to date: a joint venture with a state owned oil and gas company whose assets and organization are located in a former communist block country. The culture of this organization is deeply entrenched in command and control style management (remnants of the communist infrastructure), low moral and productivity, and poor accountability. They have been using the same techniques and people for 40 years.

Where does an entrepreneurial E&P Company begin to make good in a joint venture like this one, where their goal is to substantially increase output of their existing production? Their team is international (executives from five countries will converge on the project). The team has worked together before in various parts of the world, very successfully. Yet, this project has challenges that make the others seem relatively easy.

Before they bring in an ounce of new technology they will take up to entire year redeveloping the organization, revitalizing the moral, redistributing authority and levels of accountability, training the local management and technical staff, and building a team together with the local executive organization.

They need to tackle, among many other challenges, the following:

1. Breaking down barriers of language and culture
2. Building communication and collaboration in all directions
3. Overcoming organizational inertia with existing employees and processes
4. Overcoming tendencies to see things as "Us vs. Them"
5. Addressing Expat burn out and quality of life issues
6. Finding solutions to government requirements that impede decision making

The division head leads this group of executives and their corresponding organizations in the challenging years ahead. The team launches the operations with a four day offsite executive retreat.

The retreat begins with a SWOT analysis addressing the upcoming challenges related to the operations of the oil fields. This will help put the outcome objectives of the following days into context. The first evening, each area makes a presentation of the opportunities and concerns.

The seminar during the retreat provides the theoretical / practical training, tools, and motivation needed to increase team effectiveness. To be truly impactful, it must be constructed on the following building blocks:

- KNOWLEDGE of oneself, the other team members, the company and its purpose;
- TRUST in oneself, each other, and in company leadership;
- COMMUNICATION in all directions -- upward, downward, and laterally; and
- COLLABORATION that produces a 'win-win' environment for the individual, team, company, and the customer.

These building blocks form an important part of the seminar and employ a dual track methodology where necessary, focusing on both the individual and team aspects of effectiveness building. Both the personal and team track begin before the retreat, with the assigned pre-work, involving both personal work and executive coaching by telephone. That same executive coaching, one-on-one, will continue for the duration of the retreat.

The location for the off-site retreat is important. The preferred location would be an isolated setting (lake-view lodge or ranch) rather than a hotel. This will allow the participants to focus on the work at hand, avoid unnecessary distractions, and allow for outdoor teambuilding activities.

Deliverables

Dual track deliverables:
- Executive Team Development Program and Personal Business Plan
- Team leader (Global head of operations) will lead some interventions

Pre-work for individual development
- Executive Personality Assessment

- Executive Coaching which includes feedback from Assessment, Core Value assessment, and beginning the work toward completion of personal goals and objectives (by telephone).

<u>Pre-work for team development</u>
- Online questionnaire for each member to determine interest level, feedback on their local situation, and concerns regarding the team.
- Recommended reading is provided to executives in various locations worldwide.

This entrepreneurial, dynamic Oil and Gas Company sees teamwork and collaboration as crucial building blocks in the success of their joint venture.

We fast-forward one year, and the company has now increase production of marginal oil fields by 25% across the board, and is well on the way to transforming the work culture of their organization.

<u>Organizational Leadership</u>

This brings us to the interpretation of the word spiritual in an organizational context: *an organization that takes care of cultivating and reflecting on its role in business and society and thus fulfilling its mission.* These leaders articulate with authority, eloquence, and depth of insight. They provide deeper meanings, inspiration, and fresh insights into the human condition. They create and utilize powerful visions, metaphors, and symbols. They are the gateways for humanity to explore new facets of the future, to explore collective understanding. Spiritual visionaries pioneer new, dynamic, and flexible ways of thinking about holistic problems and questions of the world. They embody and model the search for wholeness, unity, completeness, love, peace, and fulfillment emphasizing social and spiritual responsibility toward the community, society, and the world.

WHERE WE HAVE BEEN AND WHERE WE ARE GOING

Only the strong survive. To this point in the book we have been focusing on building a business's strength—the ability of an organization to see through things; to see things through; and to see how to keep things going. These three abilities combine to continuously create unprecedented results for the business and society. This is the defining quality we postulate for effective leadership.

The Three Pyramids

Leader Pyramid
Envision: New Leadership Consciousness and Learning

Leaders need to develop profound people rapport – profound rapport is at the root of social influence. Demonstrating consciousness of others means being aware of and attuned to those with whom you are working. For the individual leader, this profound rapport with people is developed through:

a. New Consciousness – self-awareness of our nature, values and character that influence personal behavior and ultimately our effectiveness as leaders.
b. Leadership Learning – education in leadership practices and effective methods of leading others.
c. Leadership Growth - executing on goals and objectives that increase capacity to lead: developing new skills and shoring up weaknesses.

To transcend as a leader you must be able to envision a mutually desired and meaningful vision because that sets the bar. Once the bar is set the organization can align with the vision.

The Leadership Trilogy

Envision ⟶ Enable ⟶ Execute

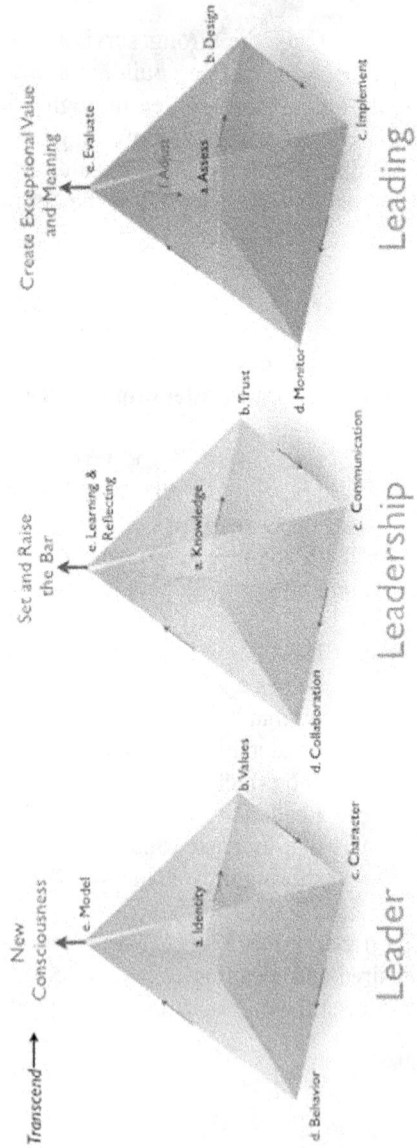

Transcend ⟶

New Consciousness

e. Model
a. Identity
b. Values
c. Character
d. Behavior

Leader

Set and Raise the Bar

e. Learning & Reflecting
a. Knowledge
b. Trust
c. Communication
d. Collaboration

Leadership

Create Exceptional Value and Meaning

e. Evaluate
a. Assess
f. Adjust
b. Design
c. Implement
d. Monitor

Leading

Leadership Pyramid – Enable: Setting and Raising the Bar

Leadership is the basic human process of enabling, maintaining, involving and connecting individuals to larger contexts such as groups, organizations communities, nations and societies. Leadership is the communal counterpart of the deeply personal process of self-understanding, as individuals, and the reasoning that goes along with being part of some whole.

Leadership occurs in many forms and arises from multiple sources. It is pervasive and not limited to formal leaders. We do not advance the traditional leader-centric model but shift the focus toward a collective and collaborative leadership approach. We have postured leadership in a cultural context. Substantial amounts of empirical research has demonstrated that what is expected of leaders, what leaders may and may not do, and the status and influence bestowed on leaders vary considerably as a result of the culture in which the leaders function. Creating a positive culture can make a significant contribution to organizational success while a negative one can lead to failure. While culture is not the only determinant of business success or failure, a positive culture can be a significant competitive advantage over organizations with which a firm competes.

In simple terms, culture defines "the shared values, beliefs and behaviors of people in social groups" (Worrall, 2009, A Climate for Change). It refers to how people think, act and get things done in your company and is comprised of three components:

1. *Experiences*, which foster beliefs
2. *Beliefs*, which influence actions
3. *Actions*, which produce results

Setting the bar anchors everything. If the organization is harmonized with what's envisioned it can move forward and the bar can keep being raised.

Leading Pyramid
Execute: Create Exceptional Meaning and Value

Execution is more than a tactic – it is a discipline and a system. It has to be built into a company's strategy and goals, and leaders of the organization must be deeply engaged in it. To that end, we have embedded an "operating system" into the organization based on mutual influence and the common purpose between leaders and collaborators. Both leader and collaborator are moved to higher levels of cooperation in order to achieve important goals.

In the operating system we describe, leaders are influenced by the collaborators in **creating exceptional value and meaning.** The coming together of value, meaning-making and people (who see themselves as part of the whole), all contribute and are critical to the process. Meaning-making is the catalyst that moves each to want to achieve desired results. The operating system also provides a framework for identification and development of more leaders. A challenge for those in top positions in large organizations is to create a collective experience that provides meaning through many interrelated and smaller collective experiences.

Leadership Trilogy - *"The person who figures out how to harness the collective genius of their organisation is going to blow the competition away."*
          Walter Wriston, former CEO Citicorp

That's what we will show you how to do next: release the collective genius of the organization, and of the world beyond the organization. Such is the power of the collective genius, of the collaborative network. It will crush any organization that stays rigid, mechanical and closed.

- Part IV -
The Ability to do Larger Things

- 8 -
Geniuses
Great Leaders and Their Organizations
Think Differently

"Let us seek with the desire to find, and find with desire to seek still more."

--Augustine of Hippo

THE INKLINGS OF NEUROSCIENCE IN A FILM LIKE AVATAR REACHES MILLIONS OF VIEWERS WHO MAY OTHERWISE HAVE HAD NO EXPOSURE TO THESE CONCEPTS THAT WILL DEFINE THE 21ST CENTURY. PHYSICAL NEUROSCIENCE GETS ITS SHARE OF THE SPOTLIGHT IN THE FILM, FROM THE FILAMENTS THAT BOND CREATURES TOGETHER TO THE UNVEILING OF THE PLANET AS A NETWORK OF TREES "COMMUNICATING LIKE NEURONS IN A BRAIN." THE TREE IS A FITTING VISUAL ANALOGY- ONE THAT FITS MODERN NEUROSCIENCE, ITS APPLICATION TO THE BUSINESS WORLD AND THE GENIUS CHARACTERISTIC.

"IT'S A NETWORK — A GLOBAL NETWORK"

JAMES CAMERON AVATAR

Science is getting ever closer to solving the complex puzzle that is the human brain. And it's beginning to look as if there's genius in all of us.

All humans have creative capacity. Each of us has a brain which weighs somewhere around 3 pounds but which is more powerful than a thousand of the most powerful computers on the planet. With all that potential, the problem is that most of us do not use this fantastic tool we are given.

Recently, new breakthroughs into research by neuroscientists have demonstrated that each of us can learn to use our brain resources more effectively. The genius is a symbol for an individual's potential: all that a person may be lies locked inside. So, when we say as leaders that we want to help people to develop their potential, we're essentially saying that we want to assist them in finding their inner genius and support them in guiding it into pathways that can lead to personal fulfillment and to the benefit of those around them.

The Leadership Trilogy

Envision   ⟶   Enable   ⟶   Execute

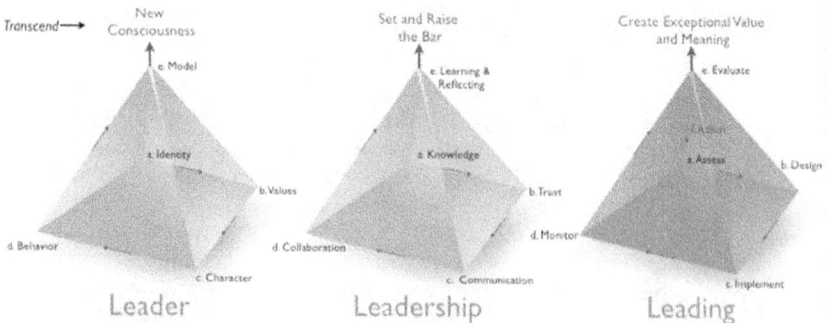

Transcend ⟶ New Consciousness

e. Model
a. Identity
b. Values
d. Behavior
c. Character

Leader

Set and Raise the Bar

e. Learning & Reflecting
a. Knowledge
b. Trust
d. Collaboration
c. Communication

Leadership

Create Exceptional Value and Meaning

e. Evaluate
a. Assess
b. Design
d. Monitor
c. Implement

Leading

The leadership trilogy is the foundation of the leadership journey - the Great Pyramid labeled Genius Network in the following illustration represents the exercising of all that has been developed in our journey at the highest level, "empowering others to achieve the extraordinary". Pixar cofounder Ed Catmull calls this the greatest form of leadership.

> The most effective leaders no longer want the job of solving their organization's biggest problems or identifying its best opportunities on their own. Instead, they recognize that the most powerful ideas can come from the most unexpected places: the quiet genius buried deep inside the organization, the collective genius that surrounds the organization, the hidden genius of customers, suppliers, and other constituencies who would be eager to share their insights if they were asked. For companies, and the CEOs at their helms, those are the smartest (and most sustainable) sources of greatness.
>
> Provided by Harvard Business Review
> "Where Leaders Get Their Edge"

Consider that everyone in an organization is not only a knowledge worker but has a creative genius. Imagine that this genius is actually a part of each human being, part of our mind. It helps us to solve issues, deal with any kind of situation, and create something new. Genius can thus be viewed as furthering the journey intimately linked with the pursuit of growth or development of the organization and its community. Leadership Genius (LG) is the capacity to focus the attention of the entire genius of an organization around its vital business objectives as well as to create and preserve value - utility, social, emotional, and spiritual – for all stakeholders and beyond.

> "Acts of individual leadership are ineffective for changing a paradigm. It is a community-building process that must challenge and transform a collective worldview."
> Michael Ray, *The New Paradigm in Business*

Genius Thinking

Although we initially presented the leadership process in sequence, Genius Thinking is best understood as a whole. As explained in the previous chapter, and the ontology at the end, our effort up to this point has been to increase the effectiveness and engagement of the "values-based knowledge organization" through a process of involvement learning. The knowledge organization operates in the domain of what is known by its people as applied to the production of specified results; their senses are trained to respond to what is known and to respond to variations thereof. "Genius" operates in the domain of training the senses to make whatever expectation(s) held possible regardless of what is or is not known in the present. As the current AT&T commercial says, "rethink possible".

> … Instead of pouring knowledge into people's heads; you need to help them grind a new set of eyeglasses so they can see the world in a new way.
>
> - JOHN SEELY BROWN

Genius Network

Unlock the power of the great pyramid; build a genius network incorporating genius thinking by everyone.

> Most organizations have a plethora of methodologies, policies, white papers, other documented best practices, etc. Making that information available to **knowledge** workers is important but incomplete. If the organization does not make those same **knowledge** workers available to one another, they are limiting the effectiveness and innovation of their workforce. Organizations that do not provide ways for their employees to connect with one another and share contextualized experience will be left behind in the 21st century way of doing business.

To foster genius thinking companywide, companies must have followed our leadership journey thus far: reduced unnecessary controls, adopted friendly reward systems, instilled new attitudes about success and failure, communicated the value of achieving future expectations, provided both the tangible and the intangible resources necessary, and led with a guide's attentiveness rather than a manager's command and control. An unbounded level of success and awakening the genius requires switching from an operating process to a different structure, a <u>contextual</u> one. Each of the following is more about dealing with the character of genius thinking rather than a step-by-step process:

a. **Vitality** is the capability to continue to grow a business with the capacity for a meaningful and purposeful existence. It's easy to follow the flow. It's easy to just keep doing what you always did. But if you don't disrupt your business model, you will never maintain growth. Markets shift. Opportunities fade. To remain vital and growing, you must move beyond what is comfortable and what everyone thinks is the right thing to do. You have to be willing to turn against the norm and open yourself and your organization to new and different things, often in new and different ways. If you want to succeed, you have to grow. And if you want to grow, you have to disrupt. You have to make it a basic fact of your organization that disruption is acceptable and possibly even desirable.

A business's *usual response* is one that would be expected. A *different response* is one that is not expected. A *radical response* is one that is out in left field.

Once you see the different and radical responses, your *business as usual* response may well look too safe and uninspiring. You might be tempted to try out an idea that is radical or different, or somewhere in between. Do things differently, either existing things better or different things altogether.

b. **Direction** – "Good thinkers do not necessarily think harder, longer, or more exactly; they have simply learned to think in directions that are more likely to be productive."--Unknown

Genius Network
Discover

Transcend ——→   Where from here

e. Abductive Inquiry

f. Fiscal & Meaning Astuteness

a. Vitality

b. Direction

d. Connectedness

c. Innovative Thinking

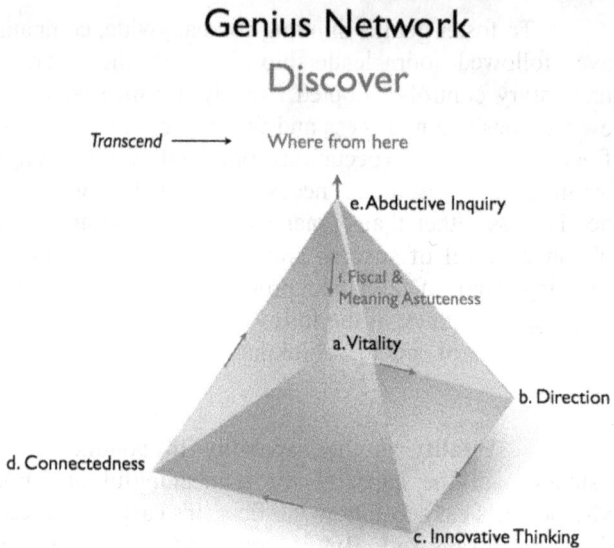

In simple situations it isn't hard to establish a better direction on the basis of discrete, conscious decisions. In more complex situations, it is often necessary to discover new directions through trial and error. New directions emerge through someone discovering a new way of doing things. New directions that emerge through trial and error are totally different from changing direction based on an all-or-nothing discrete decision. As organizational environments become increasingly complex, more and more new directions will have to emerge through trial and error (organizational learning). The leaders are those employees who, regardless of their status or influencing skills, discover new directions to pursue. Wherever complexity reigns, organizations that encourage leadership from all employees will be more successful than those that restrict leadership to managers. We use filters to select what we attend to and what we ignore. We can change the way we operate with others by changing our filters. Perspectives are ways of looking at things and we need to practice using different perspectives to increase our perceptual flexibility; frames are ways we interpret perceptions and re-framing can help us respond more resourcefully to challenges. "Directing attention is a matter of perception. If you are not looking the right direction it does not matter how clever you are, you will not see what you need to see." Edward de Bono

c. **Innovative thinking** – Innovation is creativity turned into practical action. Creativity is defined as the ability to create new ideas and things. Innovation is the application of creativity to practical problems. Another way to look at the difference is Michael Gerber's (*The E-Myth Revisited*) definition: "Creativity thinks up new things, innovation does new things." Business is obviously more interested in doing new things. The speed at which change occurs in society (and business) means the mantra for most industries is "innovate or evaporate". This explains why creativity is rapidly becoming a key factor in business success.

An IBM survey rated one leadership competency above all others: creativity. CEOs identify creativity as the most important leadership competency for the successful enterprise of the future. That's creativity, not operational effectiveness, influence, or even dedication.

The following approaches are common to the thinking styles of creative geniuses in science, art, and industry throughout history. Nine approaches to creative thinking (note the authors made a conscious effort to utilize all of these in putting together this book):

1. Rethink! Look at situations in many different ways.
2. Visualize! Utilize diagrams and imagery to analyze your dilemma.
3. Produce! Genius is productive.
4. Combine! Make novel combinations.
5. Form! Form relationships.
6. Opposite! Think in opposites.
7. Metaphor! Think metaphorically.
8. Fail! Learning from your mistakes is one way to use failure.
9. Patience! Don't confuse inspiration with ideas.

The analysis of Einstein as an OD practitioner allows the exploration of the mental models and behaviors of a nonconformist genius that broke physics paradigms and challenged conventional wisdom. Einstein is the symbol for creativity and learning. The basis for his genius was his capacity to make connections between complex things in his mind and provide a simple, yet profound explanation.

> You can use the same strategies as Aristotle and Einstein to harness the power of creativity. What teachable lessons can we learn from Albert Einstein to engage the creative mind and better manage your future? Einstein said, "Creativity is more important than knowledge."

Einstein said, "Life is like riding a bicycle; to keep your balance, you must keep moving." Einstein exercised the principles of the constructivism learning theory. This theory states that people gain knowledge and meaning from experiences, following an internal reflection process. This theory places the responsibility of learning on the individual and his ability to interact with other knowledgeable members. In his younger years, when he was working at the Patent Office, Einstein started "The Olympia Academy" that consisted of weekly meetings with his friends to discuss philosophy and physics. The Olympia Academy was the social media tool that he used to increase his learning.

Einstein placed special importance on creativity. "Creativity requires being willing not to conform, and nurturing free minds and free spirits, which in turn requires a spirit of tolerance. The underpinning of tolerance is humility: the belief that no one has the right to impose ideas or beliefs on others".

In one of his trips to America he was asked one of the famous questions from the test that Thomas Alva Edison used to apply to his employees. What is the speed of sound? He replied: "I do not know it offhand. I do not carry information in my mind that is readily available in books". He explained that the value of a college education was to train the mind to think.

d. **Connectedness** –The process of the collective mind has already been approached by a number of writers and researchers. In his book *Presence*, Otto Scharmer refers to a new type of collective relationship — one in which the individual is further enhanced rather than diminished. In Scharmer's words, the individual actually "connects...to one's highest future potential." A concern of many people when they first encounter ideas about collective genius or the collective mind is that they have to sacrifice their individuality and freedom of choice. Scharmer and the colleagues with whom he wrote *Presence* have tested this concept with a wide variety of groups and organizations. Their evidence points to the emergence of a collective mind (Sharmer's term for leadership genius (LG)) in which individuality is strengthened and enhanced rather than suppressed. Complex business development involves a large number of people from different disciplines working effectively together.

Transdisciplinary connectedness is the result of an evolution of the team approach. The transdisciplinary team model values the knowledge and skills of team members. It is dependent on effective and frequent communication among members. Members of the transdisciplinary team share knowledge, skills, and responsibilities across traditional disciplinary boundaries in assessment, planning, and execution. Transdisciplinary teamwork involves a certain amount of boundary blurring between disciplines and implies cross training and flexibility in accomplishing tasks. The essence of transdisciplinary connectedness is: by doing things together we get a better outcome than the effort done by the same amount of individuals would alone. The key point in all this should not be lost: companies that want to amplify their 'corporate brain' are smart enough to wire-up and amplify their workforce, regardless of their function, department, or rank in the development of their brain capacity by connecting and empowering more people across the entire corporate hierarchy.

Actually, some firms are now starting to use alliances to link their resources with the complementary resources of other world-class organizations. They are replacing the "not invented here" syndrome with the "invented anywhere approach" or "open innovation" as an HBS professor has labeled it. Firms are more likely to innovate when operating as a part of a strategic alliance. The innovating strategic alliance constructs a new market and become the leader from the beginning. The innovation has established a new market. If the environment adopts the innovation the firm will be the first to catch the new technology wave, this is often called first-mover advantage. A first-mover will enjoy loyalty from customers and have a huge competitive advantage. The drive to develop new markets is also known as the Blue Ocean Strategy. Blue oceans denote all the industries not in existence today, the unknown market space, untainted by competition. Innovation will lead to blue oceans; this is the market, which contains a huge opportunity for growth and profit.

> "Connectedness is a sense of being a part of something larger than oneself. It is a sense of belonging, or a sense of accompaniment. It is that feeling in your bones that you are not alone. It is a sense that, no matter how scary things may become, there is a hand for you in the dark. While ambition drives us to achieve, connectedness is my word for the force that urges us to ally, to affiliate, to enter into mutual relationships, to take strength and to grow through cooperative behavior."
>
> From the book "Connectedness", Edward M. Hallowell

"Digital transdiciplinary connectedness" is to achieve this in a virtual environment where there are no boundaries of location for the participants. Hardware, software, portals, web applications, API's, broadband connections, and so forth enable a totally new set of possibilities. We can rapidly move from old fashioned (and somewhat static) Knowledge Management software and server solutions locked into the company's IT environment toward open engines where you can both structure your input and collect your team-based output, and go far beyond that and increase work flow processes, speed up projects, and make use of your timeline far better. The most interesting discussions and biggest breakthroughs often happen at the coffee machine, or at the informal gathering. The trick is to set up a digital environment that supports common human behavior, where the technology becomes as invisible as possible. In order to achieve the optimum of all the possibilities, the most important factor is not the digital boundaries, but the organizational ability to change from an old-fashioned workflow, toward new and improved processes. Defining accurate and flexible concepts for your organizational connectedness and how to implement this in your organization can be a bigger challenge than the digital bit. Social networking was the most significant business development of 2010, topping the resurgence of the U.S. automobile industry. During the year, social networking morphed from a personal communications tool for young people into a new vehicle that business leaders are using to transform their communications with their employees and customers, as it shifts from one-way transmission of information to two-way interaction. Leaders like IBM's Sam Palmisano, PepsiCo's Indra Nooyi, Apple's Steve Jobs, Microsoft's Steve Ballmer, Carlson's Marilyn Nelson, and Harvard Business School Dean Nitin Nohria are all active social network users. Why? Because these social networks are a unique way of broadly communicating real-time messages to the audiences they want to reach. They can write a message anywhere, anytime, and share it with interested parties without any public relations meddling, speechwriters, airplane travel, canned videos, or voicemail messages. Now their words are much more authentic and can be remarkably more empowering.

Village Idiot and Collective Genius

Howard Bloom gives us a wonderful example of the power of a genius network among our closest relatives in nature. In his book, *Global Brain*, Bloom compares the behaviors of chimpanzees and baboons. Chimpanzees are more intelligent than baboons; they even make their own tools. This latter fact further highlights the development of their individual intelligence. Comparatively the baboon is the village idiot when left to operate in isolation from the pack. On the other hand, collectively baboons have achieved status as "the most widely distributed non-human primate" in Africa. In fact they have been described as the "rats of Africa", flourishing in an environment where their smarter chimp cousins are rapidly disappearing. So what are the factors contributing to the baboon's success? One of the most striking differences between chimps and baboons is that although the chimps have a more advanced brain capacity, baboons have much better developed social networks. While chimps live in groups of approximately 40, baboons congregate in troops of three to six times that size. One of the additional advantages of larger groups is that the pack provides greater protection from attack to individual members. In larger groups there is also a much more expansive social database of knowledge and, We would suggest, greater CG at work. Collaboratively baboons are geniuses when compared to the individually smarter chimp. Because of their larger network they can gather greater quantities of information about their environment and adapt to changes more rapidly. Their capacity to summon the CG within their troop has very distinct (and life saving) advantages. What baboons are achieving shouldn't really be a surprise. Our own ancestors discovered the strength-in-numbers principle very early. Picture the moment in time when our cave-dwelling ancestors figured out that taking down a hairy mammoth was going to require a large group of fairly well coordinated individuals. Even the African expression "it takes a whole village to raise a child" reminds us that people have relied upon networks to care for the precious things in life. In our modern society the importance of connection is being forgotten or lost in many places. When that occurs there is a disconnection from the collaborative genius that has served us so well throughout the evolution of our species.

e. **Abductive inquiring** – An inquiring mind must make a first step toward apprehending an experience by means of abduction, or a peculiar logic of discovery. Despite being initially pre-conscious and necessarily vague, the inference belongs to objective logic understood broadly as the laws of thought a long tradition in the history of philosophy. Abductive inquiry is a whole new way of thinking. We see traditional companies rewarding two types of logic: inductive (proving that something actually operates) and deductive (proving that something must be)." Abductive thinking combines inductive and deductive reasoning to create a fresh approach we define as "suggesting that something may be and reaching out to explore it." Instead of acting on what's certain, abductive inquiry bets on what's probable. Companies such as Apple say, "if everything must be proven, we'll never make the likes of an iPod." Abductive inquiry coupled with the transdisciplinarity is radical, in the sense that it goes to the roots of knowledge, and questions our way of thinking and our construction and organization of knowledge. It requires a discipline of inquiry that integrates the knower in the process of knowing.

f. **Fiscal and meaning astuteness** – these are core ingredients; don't proceed without them.

Cash flow is one of the most important aspects of running any business, large or small. It is one of the single most important reasons why many businesses fail - regardless of how much good the actual business is doing. Managing cash flow therefore is vitally important to the smooth-running survival and success of a business. It seems like common sense that companies should seek to be profitable. In fact, only a minority is on a consistent basis. As of the second quarter of 2009, only 23% of all public companies with revenue of $100 million to $10 billion were achieving both positive cash flow and positive sales growth. Yes, not all companies that are achieving revenue growth are profitable. The masters of exponential growth can do both: grow their revenues and achieve positive profit and cash flow. While this may seem like common sense, the small percentage of profitable-growth companies demonstrates just how difficult it is to do both.

To reiterate, it's not only profits; profitable growth with meaning is the Holy Grail we are searching for! The world we live in is increasingly complex and interconnected. Innovations and sustainable solutions to the challenges we face in our organizations and communities lie not in one leader or one viewpoint. To produce wise action and sustainable results, we need to engage the knowledge, wisdom, and capacity that are within each of our organizations, our communities, and us. In response to this need, new leadership skills and facilitation tools have evolved. They are designed to enable us to work together with intelligence and wisdom in large or small groups to create an opportunity for all voices present to be heard and listened to in a place where people are treated with respect regardless of their views. These tools create the opportunity for the wisdom in the room to emerge.

These new tools support group dialogue and conversation where the gathering is designed not as a meeting but as a harvest of ideas so that participants feel a sense of ownership in the outcomes. As you advance in your experience try additional discovery methods such as World Café, Open Space Technology, Appreciative Inquiry, Theory U, the Chaordic Stepping Stones planning process, Scenario Planning, or Technology of Participation Strategic Planning and Focused Conversations.

| Go Deeper | www.effective-leadership.com/go-deeper |

The desire to make a difference in the world

Community building, within an organization and inter-organizationally, aligned with the development of an expanding base of an applied genius network, creates the foundational elements for "social capital" —an ultimate commitment— to fostering healthy systems both within the organization itself and between the organization and the larger environment in which it lives and operates—suppliers, vendors, community, and regulatory. We describe social capital as the networks, norms, and social trust that facilitate coordination, communication, and cooperation for mutual economic and non-economic benefit (the outcome). What should we focus on? Where do we begin?

Oil is increasingly plentiful on the upslope of the bell curve, increasingly scarce and expensive on the down slope. The peak of the curve coincides with the point at which the endowment of oil has been 50 percent depleted. Once the peak is passed, oil production begins to go down while costs begin to go up.

> Food for Thought My father rode a camel. "I drive a car. My son flies a jet airplane. His son will ride a camel." a saying from oil-rich Saudi Arabia

World Oil Production 1900-2080

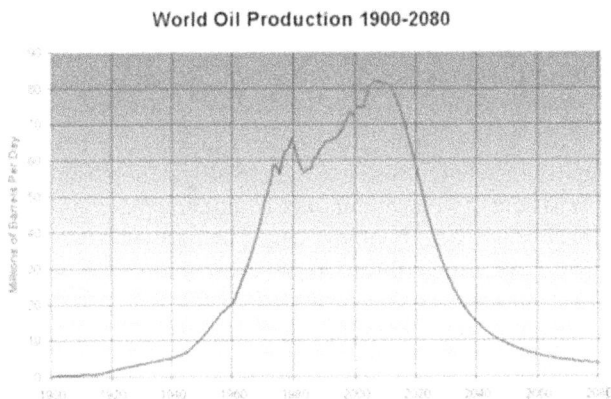

In practical and considerably oversimplified terms, this means that if 2005 was the year of global Peak Oil, worldwide oil production in the year 2030 will be the same as it was in 1980. However, the world's population in 2030 will be both much larger (approximately double) and much more industrialized (oil-dependent) than it was in 1980. Consequently, worldwide demand for oil will outpace worldwide production of oil by a significant margin.

Discover – prepare for the future

Once you have fully digested this section and are ready to act, get started by using the world oil production issue as an initial exercise since it no doubt affects everyone worldwide. Setup teams and have them choose one person in each to be responsible for keeping well-organized notes and converting the notes into paragraph form. Paragraphs work better than bullet points, as bullets points tend to give the impression of a complete list, while an open-ended paragraph leaves room for further discussion and exploration. Have the teams present their answers to the large group to see how well each honored the discipline outlined in genius thinking!

Now that you are satisfied with their work on the above effort, have them work on the series of questions below.

1. What are three reasons for wanting to adapt or grow your business?
2. What five values do you want your business to represent and grow on?
3. What do you want your business to look like ten years from now? Where will you be? What will you be doing?
4. What are the outside market conditions that may or may not have an impact on your business and growth?
5. Who are your three main competitors? What are their strengths and weaknesses?
6. What four trends in your industry impact your business the most?
7. Based on the competition, trends, and where you want to be ten years from now, how will you adapt or grow your business over the next one to three years?

- 9 -
Mastery
Heart and Soul of Leadership

"To live in hearts we leave behind is not to die."
-- Clyde Campbell

The ancients believed that the heart was the seat of the soul. In modern times, this seat has been moved from the heart to the head. Regardless of the significance we assign to our intellect or brainpower, it is just one form of intelligence. While it has an important place within our world, it is not the primary intelligence of the Self.

Our primary intelligence is empowered through emotional mastery and our ability to conduct our life from the platform of our heart. Mastery is a matter of the heart and is a precursor to success. Great organizations have a strong heart and soul. The heart and soul of any business are no different than the heart and soul of any person. The healthier the heart, the stronger the blood moves through the body. Wise organizations distinguish themselves from competitors by developing their heart. Organizations that have heart enrich their owners, customers, and communities in both economic and non-economic ways.

The truly great companies, the ones that have either broken through or redefined their industries, have one thing in common. Most often it is heart. Google, Apple, Patagonia, and

Whole Foods are just a few of the great brands with heart. In fact, heart is precisely how they got to the top.

Other benefits of creating, building, and running a heart-based company:

Heart-based companies attract the best talent – more and more today, people don't want to work for the heartless corporate behemoth. Even though there might be a lucrative corporate ladder, the sacrifice of self and values along the way isn't worth it. Companies that can provide a values-based career path secure the best talent for less. And the better the talent, the better the results.

Heart means higher purpose which means more productive employees – when people are on a mission, they will care more, they work harder and they will produce more. Companies with heart have employees that produce well beyond the norm.

Heart-based companies have more buzz –heart-based companies, when compared to ordinary mind-based companies, tend to connect better and more often with the people they serve. And as people, we tend to talk about what and who we like. That's buzz.

Heart-based companies have more loyal customers – you've probably heard it costs more to get a new customer or client than it does to sell more to the ones you have. The good news is that when you and your employees deliver your product or service with heart, the people you serve tend to stick around. That's good for business.

Heart-based companies are more valuable – a brand that is heart based has a certain magic that makes the overall company more valuable. You probably know that the greatest asset a company can have is its brand, and when created and managed with heart, your brand can bring you millions when it's time to sell your company.

Questions to Ponder

1. What's in the heart and your soul of your organization? Does your organization really have a passion for helping others (all others – stakeholders, the environment you exist in, etc.) grow and develop and reach their full potential?

2. Were your senior team members put in their positions because of their leadership ability, or because they were good at the jobs they were promoted from? Be passionately committed to effective leadership. We are never done learning. Keep a focus on continuous leadership development.

3. Can your organization engage people in a vision of a better future? Effective organizations can picture the vision of where they're headed so vividly that everyone can feel it and can imagine him or herself in it.

4. Are you making it about everyone? Bringing out the best in people entails, on the part of everyone involved, hard work, clear communication, cultivation of job skills, and a dedication to practical processes.

When you come to understand that leadership is not just about compelling people to act in certain ways but helping them bring out the best in themselves, you'll make big advances in your organizations effectiveness.

5. Are you willing to rock the status quo, to step out of the comfort zone, and be creative and innovative? If the imperative is not getting far more results than ever before, don't heed the call; stick with the old leadership methods.

Go
Deeper   www.effective-leadership.com/go-deeper

Leadership Genius Unpacked
Effective action for social influence

In describing how leadership genius is deployed, we discover seven actions that are constituent parts of a larger whole, a *system of social influence,* whose parts are interrelated and depend upon one another. "Effectiveness is doing the right things" Peter Drucker.

Seven Actions of Leadership Genius

1. Catalyst Action: The Individual
2. Orchestrating Action: The Group
3. Operative Action: The Organization
4. Viral Action: Across Organizations
5. Meaningful Action: Governance
6. Virtuous Action: All Stakeholders
7. Future Sight Action: For the survival of all

1. Catalyst Action: The Individual

1. Transcending as a model leader to a <u>Profound Rapport with people</u> – This is the heart of the first component of leadership genius. Profound rapport is the "Relationship of mutual trust and emotional affinity."
2. The way in which you interact with others has a major bearing on your success as an influencer; building rapport is the catalyst for influencing others. It is vital if you wish to maintain relationships. Without it, you are unlikely to achieve willing agreement. People who have excellent rapport with others create harmonious relationships based on trust and understanding of mutual needs.

3. A Recipe For Successful Influence:

   <u>Ingredients:</u>
   Trust
   Openness
   Comfort level

Acceptance
Empathy
Something in common
Shared understanding

4. Method:
Mix together ingredients as needed. In building rapport with another, take note of how the person responds. We often live in a bubble, taking little notice of how others react to the things we say and do. Do we make others feel uncomfortable by the way we express ourselves? Are we repeat offenders in this, doing nothing to modify our words and actions to build deeper rapport? Self-reflection and discipline are the only answers here. One must think at two levels simultaneously – the first being our own thought process and self-expression, the second being that of constantly observing the response/reaction of others (both verbally and non-verbally). Can we think at two levels at once? We can and must become masters of this. Much can be learned in building rapport through our daily interaction with others.

Self-Disclosure:
Letting others know what we think, how we feel about an issue, and sharing our beliefs and background is a type of currency. If we share information about ourselves we usually will receive more in return. People tend to group together by type, background, interests, beliefs, gender, work, and so forth. One of the most efficient ways to build rapport is through self-disclosure. As we begin to experience a common bond, so too does rapport begin. Mutual interests, ideas, values, and beliefs are all part of effective social interaction.

Biographic Matching:
It is rare for two human beings to be together for very long before seeking to discover similarities between themselves. This biographic matching can be social or economic – achieved through outlook, education or background – common experiences of the world. When you match, you reduce resistance by playing down differences while building upon similarities.

Pacing:

Similar to Matching is Pacing. The latter is a dynamic continuation of the first. Pacing is maintaining the rhythm that is being created through mutual agreement, seeing things from the same point of view. Pacing is a conscious continuation of matching through the ongoing building of common ground.

When talking, you can pace:
- Words that are used
- Tone of voice
- Language patterns
- Volume
- Body language used

We note that many times matching, pacing and self-discloser are done without much thought, and some individuals are much better than another in attaining deeper rapport. We need to be aware of how proficient we are at this. Self-awareness is key here. In earlier chapters we reviewed our personality derailers – the aspects of our personality that appear when under pressure or stress that often have an effect on our ability to relate well with others. They are stumbling blocks for matching and pacing.

Leading:

One of the goals of matching and pacing is to be able to lead another in a different direction, a more positive one that benefits both the individual and the organization. When rapport is present, relationship are in sync, and a change of pace from you will usually result in a similar change in others. Matching and pacing help you to share your experience and expertise with others by ultimately leading others to a better future. Over time, with practice, one begins to intuitively know when it is appropriate to make suggestions, to influence, or to lead.

Mismatching:

You can also influence behavior in others by mismatching. It is useful to mismatch when:

- You want a meeting to come to an end – clear up papers, put a pen away
- You want to conclude a telephone conversation – minimize responses.
- You need time to think before acting – use the bathroom, make a telephone call, add up figures on your calculator.
- When what you are doing isn't working – go for a walk, listen to some music, make a phone call.
- Matching is affecting your mood negatively – break off the conversation, change the subject.

Networking:

Have you noticed how some people seem to be universally liked, trusted, and respected? Chances are that they're also good at networking – developing a wide network of friends, colleagues, allies, and useful contacts. Networking offers you a structured way to make certain that <u>your ideas are effectively exchanged with others.</u> This is key to extending your influence.

After a decade at the helm of Campbell Soup, Douglas R. Conant established a reputation as a leader capable of delivering big profits and strategic change. The key to transformative leadership, he says, is to ensure that everyone in your organization knows your goals and feels included. "Ninety-nine out of a hundred times I'm not in the room when decisions are made - it's other people," he says. "If you want them to value your agenda ... they have to know you value their agenda as individuals."

2. Orchestrating Action: The Group

1. The primary goal of a leader is to produce more leaders. "The substance of the leader's job is to produce more collaborative leaders, not more followers".

2. All Great Leaders are *collaborative*. Facilitation might be considered an advanced form of collaboration. The leader as facilitator must ensure that the internal structural and operational systems are aligned with the core values of the organization. It is such alignment that builds trust in the integrity of the leader and the organization. Leading and influencing is no easy matter. It requires a high level of training, skill, patience, and perseverance to see the process through to completion. It is an especially important role. In assuming it the leader is reminded that leadership is not a solo act. It involves the capacity to work with others. When the leader's role includes that of facilitator, it builds the capacity of others and increases the chances of success. This is the Leadership Model of the future.

3. Being a collaborative leader is more about asking the right questions than giving the right answers – more about guiding than giving orders. By definition a leader is a person who guides or inspires others: a facilitator is a person who directs, assists, and stimulates. The similarities are obvious. This does not suggest that a leader should or can always assume this role effectively. It is therefore critical to the success and the well being of the group that leaders be cognizant of appropriate facilitation opportunities and limitations. One may argue with neutrality but the greatest leaders were great because they also listened to their people.

4. The art of questioning and listening – effective questioning requires it be combined with effective listening. Effective questions are questions that are powerful and thought provoking. Effective questions are open-ended and non-leading questions. They are not "why" questions, but rather "what" or "how" questions. "Why" questions are good for soliciting information, but can make people defensive so be thoughtful in your use of them. When asking effective questions, it is important to wait for the answer and do not provide the answer.

When working with people, it is not enough to tell them what you want. They need to find out or understand for themselves. You help them do this by asking them thought provoking questions. Rather than make assumptions find out what the person you are talking to knows. Behind effective questioning is also the ability to listen to the answer and suspend judgment. This means being intent on understanding what the person who is talking is really saying. What is behind their words? Let go of your opinions so that they don't block your learning more information. Pay attention to your gut for additional information.

Leaders who follow the path toward leadership genius say they spend 50% or more of their time listening. Listening is a core leadership skill. How much time do you spend listening to the views of others - employees, peers, customers, or other stakeholders? How effective are you at it? Although listening is considered a *soft skill,* it produces hard results in relationship building.

The following summarizes listening skills that every leader should practice. They involve the art of active listening and the barriers to effective listening.

Listening as a Core Leadership Skill

Listening is critical for leadership success because it enables effective relationships. We have found that listening:

- Demonstrates respect for others and their ideas
- Fosters reciprocal listening
- Engenders trust
- Fosters better relationships with employees
- Promotes employee autonomy and creativity
- Manages the expectations of others

These are particularly important during times of exceptional change (merger, acquisition, downsizing, or rapid growth). The more stress an organization is facing, the more important it is for its leaders to demonstrate soft skills such as listening to and empathizing with employees who are facing workplace upheaval.

A report in Fortune Magazine revealed that approximately 40% of senior leaders fail in their jobs within the first 12-18 months. A prime cause is the failure to establish effective working relationships. Lou Gerstner, who led IBM's revival, provided an account of his first month at IBM. In his book, *Who Says Elephants Can't Dance,* Gerstner said before establishing his priorities for IBM's future, "For the first month, I listened, and I tried very hard not to draw conclusions."

To help leaders effectively assimilate into a new environment, some companies provide programs in *Executive Onboarding.* These programs are designed to help executives establish solid working relationships with key internal and external stakeholders. For a senior executive, effective use of the first 3 months on the job is crucial for future success. Components of the onboarding program can include a two-day onboarding session where the executive team and the incumbent collaborate closely with an outside facilitator to understand concerns, cultural barriers, expectations, leadership styles, and personalities. The facilitator works separated with both executives and teams, later bringing them together to build bridges. Onboarding programs can also include executive coaching during the first six months of the new hire, providing feedback as well as supporting execution of key goals and objectives.

Key skills to Practice for Effective Listening

Leaders are encouraged to practice two fundamental skills of effective listening: paraphrasing and listening with empathy.

Paraphrasing is a skill that good communicators use to:
- Draw out speakers and make them feel heard and understood,
- Neutralize a loaded attack
- Understand the meaning behind words.

Paraphrasing forces the listener to slow down and hear what the speaker is saying. It gives both the listener and the speaker the assurance that the intended thought and feeling are conveyed.

Listening with empathy entails listening for content as well as feelings. Facilitators use this technique to ensure meetings are productive for everyone involved. Great leaders generally are good facilitators because they are good listeners.

Listening Filters
The thoughts and ideas we bring into a conversation filter what we hear. It happens naturally and usually subconsciously. Part of a key to listening effectively (and also effectively mentoring others) is to be able to place us ourselves in the other person's shoes, listening from their perspective. Listening filters can keep us from doing this effectively. They become barriers to good communication. Listed below are 7 common filters.

1. Self-Interests
2. Attitudes
3. Values
4. Expectations
5. Current mood
6. Prejudices
7. Assumptions

Leaders who recognize their own listening filters are better able to follow Stephen Covey's advice, "Seek first to understand, then to be understood.

The questioning and listening approach described would be the antithesis of Reality Distortion Field (RDF), a term coined by Burrell Smith at Apple Computer in 1981, to describe the company's co-founder Steve Jobs' charisma and its effect on the developers working on the Mac project. Bud Tribble claimed that the term came from Star Trek. Later the term has also been used to refer to perceptions of his keynote speeches (or "Stevenotes") by observers and devoted users of Apple computers and products.

The RDF is said by Andy Hertzfeld to be Steve Jobs' ability to convince himself and others to believe almost anything with a mix of superficial charm, charisma, bravado, hyperbole, marketing, appeasement, and persistence. RDF is said to distort an audience's sense of proportion and scales of difficulties and to make them believe that the task at hand is possible.

3. Operative Action: The Organization

We take our cue from musical theory where *consonance* is a harmony, chord or interval is considered stable, as opposed to *dissonance,* which is considered to be unstable (or temporary transitional). Consonance is a combination of notes that sound pleasant to most people when played at the same time where dissonance is a combination of notes that sound harsh or unpleasant.

1. Cognitive – Consonance and Dissonance have a similar meaning to their musical counterpart. Cognitive Consonance is a state of harmony and internal consistency (stability) arising from compatibility among a person's attitudes, behaviors, beliefs, and/or knowledge. Cognitive dissonance is the opposite and describes the uncomfortable tension that may result from having two conflicting thoughts at the same time or engaging in behavior that conflict with one's beliefs.
2. In popular usage, it can be associated with the tendency for people to resist the acceptance and assimilation of information that is in some way in conflict with current understanding. This cognitive dissonance may invite them to act in ways that depart from their current mode of thinking.
3. This affects almost every aspect of people's lives. The awareness of it and response to it will influence whether or not people learn, or grow and change in some of their views.
4. As a positive driving force, cognitive dissonance causes us to think creatively when solving problems, however, it becomes negative when we rationalize bad situations and accept them, as the way things have to be. The Habit of Leadership Genius acquired here involves creating and encouraging cognitive consonance most of the time, and occasionally causing dissonance in order to break with old paradigms and to stimulate creativity.

4. Viral Action: Inter-Organizational Networks

A. Globalization is becoming a business imperative in most industries for both survival and growth. The most commonly used measure of leader effectiveness is the extent to which the leader's organizational unit performs its task successfully and attains its goals.

B. However, the fluidity and globalization exhibited by many organizations suggest that leadership effectiveness in the future may be measured on a leader's ability to lead a network, not a group or unit.

C. Successful development and administration of inter-organizational networks is derived from effective intercultural communication efforts focused on developing relationships. Intercultural Communicative Competence has been said to combine three components:

- Knowledge - information necessary to interact appropriately and effectively
- Positive affirmation – for example, positive affect toward the other culture, empathy
- Skills - behavior necessary to interact appropriately and effectively

D. **Integrating mechanisms** are essential if such networks are to be effective in coordinating the work of a diverse range of partners. Importantly, they are required for the development of trust. Therefore, the literature stresses that trust between the parties is central to the effective operation of such networks.

5. Meaningful Action: Governance

1. In a 2007 study, Sean Griffith and Tom Baker examined how liability insurers transmit and transform the content of corporate and securities law. The findings suggest that what matters in corporate governance are deep governance variables such as culture and character, rather than the formal governance structures that are typically studied. Corporate culture is a profound driver of any business – it determines the company's ability to execute its strategic vision and

mission. Leadership and corporate culture excellence are essential to company performance and organizational well being. The "tone at the top" shapes corporate culture and drives organizational behavior, which pervades internal and external relationships.

The Board of Directors is the steward of the corporate soul, the spirit of success.
"The soul of an enterprise is the tie that binds, the furnace of passion, the cauldron of commitment, the acceptance of accountability, the vista of visions, and the belief that what is being done is being done for the right reasons."

-    *Bob McDonald's Blog on Business*

2. Corporate performance depends on the support of their boards. The board's role as much as oversight should include helping develop additional income streams, new capabilities, and fresh intellectual capital. They invest in director development and the professional selection, appointment, and induction of new directors. Their chairmen need to consciously build effective boards of competent directors.
3. The failure for many has been the preoccupation with ensuring compliance rather than having the fortitude or foresight to align their organizations in taking effective action to truly increase business value.
4. What's **needed is to improve the competence of directors and the effectiveness of boards** to support **meaningful** action **that begets successful results. In a study** of the effectiveness of 2500 companies' boards it was reported: "Every one of over 2,500 firms participating in the study could significantly increase individual achievements and corporate performance" Prof. Colin Coulson-Thomas author of 'Winning Companies"

"Good corporate governance can be a competitive advantage if the board focuses on performance, *not conformance*." A basic plan for directors would require them to hire and evaluate the chief executive and monitor the strategic plan with clear milestones. The board should also be involved in succession plans, internal development and pay-for-performance. Board members also should be evaluated, the way executives are. Only 20% of corporate directors face performance measures." David W. Johnson, chairman and CEO emeritus of Campbell Soup Co.

Go Deeper   www.effective-leadership.com/go-deeper

6. Virtuous Action: Stakeholders

The first step is to go back to the beginning of our discussion about leadership found in the first chapter of this book. Being a master of self is the first defining step. Benjamin Franklin, notable as a statesman and scholar brings some insight into the subject of self-mastery.

As Odysseus famously puts it in Dante's Inferno, "Fatti non foste per viver come bruti, ma per seguir virtute e canoscenza" (We were not made to live like brutes, but to follow virtue and knowledge).

Benjamin Franklin
Leadership by Virtue

1. **Temperance** - eat not to dullness; drink not to elation.
2. **Silence** - Speak not but what may benefit others or yourself; avoid trifling conversation.
3. **Order** - Let all your things have their places; let each part of your business have its time.
4. **Resolution** - Resolve to perform what you ought; perform without fail what you resolve.
5. **Frugality** - Make no expense but to do good to others or yourself; that is, waste nothing.
6. **Industry** - Lose no time; be always employed in something useful; cut off all unnecessary actions.
7. **Sincerity** - Use no hurtful deceit; think innocently and justly; speak accordingly.
8. **Justice** - Wrong none by doing injuries; or omitting the benefits of your duty.
9. **Moderation** - Avoid extremes; forbear resenting injuries so much as you think they deserve.
10. **Cleanliness** - Tolerate no uncleanliness in body, clothes, or habitation.
11. **Tranquility** - Be not disturbed at trifles or at accidents common or unavoidable.
12. **Chastity** - Rarely use venery but for health or offspring, never to dullness, weakness, or the injury of your own or another's peace or reputation

---

7. Future Sight ™: For the survival of all

1. We use the same concepts covered in previous chapters to engage our people in developing insights into a business's future: a structured process for giving people exposure to various future sight information. Job rotations provide an opportunity for budding leaders to gain much needed insight, but rotation must

be accompanied with real time challenges – challenges to solve critical business problems that would stretch their imagination. To meet the challenges thrown at them future leaders must be encouraged to experiment and keep what works. This not only enriches their experience but also enkindles their inquisitiveness.

Experimentation requires judicious guidance from the incumbent leaders – judicious because leaders should never over-manage. By the same token they must be able to say "stop" in spite of sunk costs and egos involved. Finally, openness in the organization to debate one's viewpoint with peers and team, building upon their ideas, is an essential enabler for gaining practical insights into the business.

2.   It all boils down to the job of leadership to create the environment that anticipates the opportunities and threats that face an organization. To create an appropriate organizational influence method, a vision statement should be crafted to help propel the organization in the right direction. To ignore the future is to fail as a leader. The wakeup call: you need to set your own future; the future is not fixed in the past. Marry the wisdom of the past with the best knowledge you can muster up today!

3.   It is essential that leaders develop *future sight* as it has the power and potential of sustaining their industry. Without this the organization is deprived of the opportunity of receiving important clues about the future before it actually arrives. In other words, opportunity to create market leadership positions in the future is lost. Leaders with future sight can put their organization ahead of the competition by changing direction and thus charting a path for their own future.

General Motors was once the largest corporation in the USA and the single largest employer in the world. It was once a common expression: "What's good for General Motors is good for the country".

"The present is always a little unsatisfying compared to the past"
- Midnight in Paris

As president of General Motors when Eisenhower tapped him to become secretary of defense in 1953, "Engine Charlie" Wilson voiced at his Senate confirmation hearing what was then the conventional view. When asked whether he could make a decision in the interest of the USA that was adverse to the interest of GM, he said he could.

Then he reassured them that such a conflict would never arise. "I cannot conceive of one because for years I thought what was good for our country was good for General Motors, and vice versa. Our company is too big. It goes with the welfare of the country."

Wilson was only slightly exaggerating. At the time, the fate of GM was inextricably linked to that of the nation. In 1953, GM was the world's biggest manufacturer – the symbol of US economic might. It generated 3% of US gross national product. GM's expansion in the 1950s was credited with stalling a business slump. It was also America's largest employer, with over 460,000 employees. Its blue-collar workers received (in today's dollars) $60 an hour that year in wages and benefits.

General Motors was the largest and most profitable U.S. Corporation. In its heyday — roughly the late 1950s to the mid 1970s — sales amounted to about 2%. And it was not just the largest manufacturer of cars — but also of heavy trucks, locomotives, and military equipment. It was a major player in aircraft production, and in household appliances — and the GM Acceptance Corporation was by far the largest retail credit institution in the United States. Like Wal-Mart today, GM had no competition that could threaten its supremacy. The tempo and cadence of the business in terms of design, engineering, segmentation, marketing, and advertising - even right down to the color palette seen on America's vehicles - Chevrolet was the straw that stirred the drink and GM completely dominated the American market.

Few organizations in American industry have had the long-term success that GM enjoyed. It was the industry's low-cost producer, with powerful economies of scale and market share as high as 60%. The impact of auto manufacturer General Motors on American culture, the economy, and politics is staggering, as is the sheer size of the corporation. For years, GM was the largest corporation on earth, its value greater than most nations. It was the first company to gross more than one billion dollars a year. When GM had a bad year in 1957, commentators said, "GM sneezed and the economy caught a cold," Controlling more than half of the market and creating more cars than its domestic rivals combined, GM made and sold cars everywhere in the world. Although regulation, foreign competition, and oil shocks have rocked GM the past few decades, for most of its history it has towered over not just the auto industry, but all industries. And from the farmer-friendly, half-ton pick-ups of the 1930s, to the luxurious Cadillac Coup De Villes or the space-age looking Buick LeSabre of the 1950s, to the Pontiac GTO for the youth longing for "muscle cars" in the late 1950s, to the "uniquely American" 1957 Chevy, to sports cars like the Pontiac Trans-Am of the 1970s, to the one and only Chevy El Camino half car/half pick-up of the same decade, GM has produced not just cars, but symbols of American culture.

Following his graduation from Virginia Tech, the author worked for ten years at General Motors Corporation during the 1960s to the early 1970s - its glory days. He was hired into GM as a college graduate trainee and put on the fast track to senior management. There was a great continuing education program. It was possible to complete advanced degrees, and the opportunity to improve one's skills was encouraged.

GM was a wonderful place in the 1960s and you were proud to say you worked there. People worked very hard and took great pride in their work. Quality and perfection were a way of life. There was true teamwork. The author really loved GM; we were a family. It was truly a great place to work and to grow as a person. Many life lessons were learned and the development of a passion for excellence that led to the desire to go out and share the experience with the rest of the world was learned there.

The later failure of General Motors and its leadership is as astounding and momentous (and ironic) as the company's early achievement. How did the board and management of a great company ever allow this extraordinary situation to develop? It is easy to point to the labor agreements from the 1950's, and the slow response to the superior engineering and manufacturing of Japanese competitors, and a reluctance to take environmental issues seriously. But these were not overnight developments. Beyond that, did GM's financial controls become too powerful a force for the product engineers to overcome? Did the marketers not see what Toyota was doing with the Camry and Lexus? Or was it simply the fact that the culture that made it great was not preserved? Only the best-prepared and managed companies survive the onslaught of the future, whatever it brings. Consider how one of the greatest leaders of our times – Jack Welch – had prepared his company for the future even before it arrived during the early 1980s. He described the winners of the future by insisting that companies hanging on the ways of the 1980s will not be around in the 1990s and thus spelled his vision of being "No.1 or 2 – fix, sell, or close". And from that future sight flowed a series of changes in the structure, portfolio, and culture of the conglomerate that by the 1990s, GE was one of the most competitive companies on the planet. It found it riding confidently on the waves of globalization when other companies were caught unprepared in uncharted waters.

4. Right Action is the essence of Leadership Genius – being able to know and do the right things (action) at the right time is <u>FutureSight</u>. The GM story reflects the undulating cycle explained in chapter 5, a cycle of great growth, then peaking and dropping, unfortunately without an intervention to align with the inevitable wave of changes in the environment in which the business operates. The "renewal" effort inevitably requires doing things differently than in the past, this is what we and Peter Drucker call "doing the right things"- only time will tell if the action is right and that too has to be timely dealt with.

Go
Deeper   www.effective-leadership.com/go-deeper

Many business owners feel that they are stuck with their business model. They say things like, "Hey, we have been in the plumbing business for 67 years, it's just the way things are." This could not be more untrue. Think about how many times IBM has fundamentally changed their business model. IBM started in 1911 selling time recording machines. That model stopped working so they shifted to the typewriter market. Then they moved into the mainframe computer market. They hit problems and refocused on consulting services. Today, IBM's model includes green consulting and city planning. These services are a far cry from typewriters and office machines.

IBM has done what many businesses have not. They have proactively changed their business model before it failed. IBM has maintained a good future focus. By focusing on the continuity of their business model, They have insured their ongoing success. What you can learn from IBM is that your current business model is only useful today. It may or may not be useful next year. Most businesses do not need to gut their model as IBM has. IBM understands that business models erode over time. Buyer behaviors change, technology makes products obsolete, and competitors enter our markets. These factors and more play into the strength of our business model. From time to time, we need to reassess our model and adjust.

Jim Muehlhausen
Author "The 51 Fatal Business Errors and How to Avoid Them"

Pyramid Symbolism

This ancient and powerful symbol has general meaning for all and specific meaning for the aspiring. It represents the coming together of the world of man with that of God, the material with the spiritual. The purpose of the pyramids was to bury the dead and to assist them into reaching eternity. In this way, the pyramids were holy places and their architecture and mysticism continues to amaze and to intrigue us. In order to understand its symbolism, consider your current accomplishments and breakthroughs. If you accomplished a personal goal and feel a sense of wholeness, this symbol of aspiration may be an affirmation of those feelings. The pyramid could also represent larger organizational goals and deepest striving. Whether they represent fulfilled or incomplete goals, a pyramid seems to be a very positive symbol for those who aspire to new heights professionally or personally.

The Great Pyramid of Giza is one of the most geometrically perfect structures ever built on planet Earth. You can find books, careers, even entire lives devoted to theories about how it was built and what its intended purpose was. However, even if you're a first time onlooker, whether in person or in a photograph, one thing is blatantly obvious–the top seems to be missing. No one has been able to explain why the Great Pyramid would have been built without a capstone. It's hard to imagine going to that enormous amount of time and effort and not topping it out; unless it was left uncompleted intentionally...for a special generation of humankind to finish the job at an appropriate time in a distant future age.

Using the pyramid analogy above and the notion that the capstone was left off intentionally, to be installed at a future time when there is a realization of a new vision; so it is with our book. Our book is not finished; our intention was to create the foundation for Leadership Genius. Those geniuses, who have the receptivity or keen observation to allow them to discover new dimensions for dealing with the challenges of tomorrow and who will eventually put a "capstone" on the work we started.

NASA symbolic imagery of unfinished pyramid

"Go Deeper" Online Resources

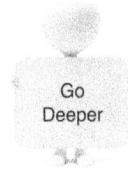
Go Deeper

We are jump-starting the process with the *Go Deeper* selections that helped inspire some of the book's content. We are constantly researching for new leadership concerns and suggestions. We will continually update the *Go Deeper Online* with relevant information; readers are welcomed to inquire any time about leadership questions they have. *Go Deeper Online* can be found at www.effective-leadership.com/go-deeper.

Self-awareness
By Vincent Higgins

"Knowing others is wisdom, knowing yourself is Enlightenment."
- Lao Tzu

What is self-awareness? The Oxford Dictionary describes self-awareness as: conscious knowledge of one's own character, feelings, motives, and desires.

In a <u>leadership culture</u> all individuals lead, inspire and influence others in order to realize the collective vision of the organization. Said another way, the organization needs to think of leadership as a distributed process and depend upon leadership behavior by every individual at every level rather than a single act reserved for individuals at the executive level. This reasoning and approach puts a high demand upon people in key leadership roles. They must look at one of their responsibilities to be that of coaching others to become more effective leaders. It is not so much that everyone will find themselves in a traditional leadership or supervisory role, but rather that they understand the attributes and traits of an effective leader and can use good leadership skills when needed.

This assessment has been taken by hundred of executives as the beginning to a deeper self-awareness, and as a platform to set goals and objectives, to be developed over time, together with an executive coach. Take about 5 minutes with each of these values, taking a few notes if necessary, and thinking about how they apply to your work life, home life and social environment. Rate yourself on each. See where you scored highest and lowest. Then, choosing two, do a SWOT analysis with each of the two. Don't choose the two values where you score the lowest, but rather choose two where you would most wish to see improvement over the next few months, taking into account current and future activities and responsibilities. Afterwards, look for a good executive coach!

The core values are divided into two categories, business and individual. In the section that follows you will identify two core values, one from each category. Spend some time reflecting on each of the core values below, and rate yourself on each.

Never	Less likely	50/50	Most likely	Always	
1	3	5	7	9	10 ___

Business

Excellence

The pursuit of distinction in business, family and community
- Insists on excellence in all things and sets the example
- Provides recognition beyond wins and billability
- Makes objective, quality service to the client a top priority; sets the example
- Continuously strives to improve work processes, products, and services
- Provides timely effective, accurate, and constructive performance feedback to team
- Recruits and develops quality staff with potential
- Contributes to and stays current with developments in the field

Teamwork

Mutual collaboration to reach common objectives without focus on personal again
- Builds strong and positive working relationships
- Maintains positive work climate
- Involves others in planning activities and decisions
- Makes optimum use of input from others
- Helps others
- Encourages, recognizes, and celebrates success of team and its members
- Supports career mobility
- Engenders enthusiasm and excitement for the work and the future
- Rewards appropriate team behavior

Entrepreneurship
Turning opportunity into success through prudent action
- Accepts and rewards risk taking in order to pursue opportunities that will benefit overall team
- Encourages creative thought and action
- Capitalizes on opportunities created by changes in the market
- Inspires with a compelling vision of the future
- Demonstrates motivation to take on new responsibilities and learn new skills

Service
Adding value through conscience effort and personal leadership
- Holds client services and the client's interest as a top priority
- Considers long-term client needs as well as short-term demands
- Makes and delivers on commitment
- Takes personal responsibility for improving service

Diversity
Appreciation for the value of differences
- Respects cultural and individual differences
- Is inclusive in work activities
- Recognizes and utilizes different perspectives when making decisions
- Does not discriminate

Influence
Moving others to think and act uprightly through conscious effort
- Taking time out to reflect on leadership style and effectiveness
- Ongoing awareness of one's strengths, weaknesses, and leadership opportunities
- Holding oneself personally accountable to positively influence and develop others
- Mentoring and coaching others to maximize their effectiveness

Individual

Professionalism
Empowering self and others to maximize effectiveness
- Seeks out and listens to honest feedback from others
- Gives candid and constructive feedback to others
- Identifies and takes opportunities to maintain/increase skills
- Takes future organizational needs into account in planning own development
- Shares own expertise and experience
- Actively supports, mentors, and coaches others

Fairness
Giving others their due in word and deed
- Consistent in treatment of staff
- Distributes information as equally as appropriate
- Uses an inclusive work and decision process
- Adheres to firm's standards
- Does not play favorites
- Recognizes the merits of individuals and their performances

Integrity
Consistency between what one professes to be and how one lives
- Keeps commitments and promises
- Demonstrates the courage to present and hear the truth in an appropriate manner
- Acts in the best interests of the client, the firm, and the team
- Displays and reinforces the highest ethical standards
- Accurately represents one's own competencies

Respect
Esteeming others by extending the same courtesy with which one hopes to be afforded
- Practices patient and active listening
- Is sensitive to other people's time
- Recognizes and credits the contributions of others
- Is empathetic to other's motivations and feelings
- Supports work/life balance needs of staff and self
- Treats others with dignity
- Shows patience, tolerance, and concern for people at all levels and from all backgrounds

Trust
Building confidence through insightful action
- Promotes open communication
- Builds trust by being honest, fair, and consistent
- Sets example for others
- Keeps confidences and information at the appropriate levels
- Accepts and acts on open and honest feedback
- Does what is right even if it involves risk or conflict
- Takes responsibility for actions and admits mistakes

Self-Mastery
Controlling one's passions amid personal drive
- Exercises self-constraint in times of strong passions
- Delays words and actions when excited to anger, frustration, or discouragement
- Steps back from situations when compelling strong emotions are present in others.

This section will help you assess your development and put a plan into place. It does so by focusing on one of the core values most in need of attention, reviewing both the internal and personal status on life relating to that core value, and the external and environmental conditions and circumstances that affect growth in that area.

1. For the *SWOT* analysis regarding the business category, choose one of these six core values: *Excellence, Teamwork, Entrepreneurship, Service, Diversity, Influence*

2. For the *SWOT* at the individual level, choose one of these six core values: *Professionalism, Fairness, Integrity, Respect, Trust,* and *Self Mastery*

Core Value (business category): _____

Strengths (positive internal and personal traits, values, resources...)

_____

_____

Weaknesses (negative internal and personal traits, vices, shortcomings, attitudes, motives)

_____

_____

Opportunities (positive external and environmental conditions and resources)

_____

_____

Threats (negative external and environmental temptations, risks and roadblocks)

_____

_____

Core Value (individual category): _____

Strengths *(positive internal and personal traits, values, resources…)*

_____

_____

Weaknesses *(negative internal and personal traits, vices, shortcomings, attitudes, motives)*

_____

_____

Opportunities *(positive external and environmental conditions and resources)*

_____

_____

Threats *(negative external and environmental temptations, risks and roadblocks)*

_____

_____

Social Power and the Coming Corporate Revolution
David Kirkpatrick, Contributor to Forbes ONLINE

Social Power and the Coming Corporate Revolution suggests a bright future for business and society globally. The world is becoming more democratic and reflective of the will of ordinary people. And pragmatically, social power can help keep your company vital. Newly armed customer and employee activists can become the source of creativity, innovation and new ideas to take your company forward. A growing number of executives and companies are converts to this point of view.

This social might is now moving toward your company. We have entered the age of empowered individuals, who use potent new technologies and harness social media to organize themselves.

But most are ordinary people with new tools to force you to listen to what they care about and to demand respect. Both your customers and your employees have started marching in this burgeoning social media multitude, and you'd better get out of their way—or learn to embrace them.

In this new world of business, companies and leaders will have to show authenticity, fairness, transparency and good faith. If they don't, customers and employees may come to distrust them, to potentially disastrous effect. Customers who don't like a product can quickly broadcast their disapproval. Prospective employees don't have to take your word for what life is like at your company—they can find out from people who already work there. And long time loyal employees now have more options to launch their own, more fleet-footed start-ups, which could become your fiercest competitors in the future.

But overall these changes suggest a bright future for business and society globally. The world is becoming more democratic and reflective of the will of ordinary people. And pragmatically, social power can help keep your company vital. Newly armed customer and employee activists can become the source of creativity, innovation and new ideas to take your company forward. A growing number of executives and companies are converts to this point of view.

The Organization of the Future?
By Dave Pollard
www.howtosavetheworld.ca

I spent the day at an interesting symposium on the Organization of the Future put on by the Boyden Institute and hosted by Steelcase Canada. The objective of the session was to envision the organization of the future, define the principles it would operate under, and begin to explore what it would take to get there.

Here are some of the elements of the picture that the participants painted:
- an organization less like an army (hierarchical, focused on winning) and more like a family/community (collaborative, focused on well-being of members) than today's large organizations
- better able to deal with complexity
- has a flexible definition of 'work' that is purposeful and meaningful to its people
- is accessible, inclusive and diverse
- is responsive to the communities it operates in
- is self-managed, innovative and entrepreneurial
- generates deep mutual respect and trust in its people
- is resilient and agile, and capable of 'acting in the moment'
- attracts people skilled at collaboration and inclined to work collaboratively
- has a self-determined, shared set of values
- is committed to "not being evil"
- is amoeba-like (permeable borders, good sensors, able to change shape when necessary, a strong guiding nucleus, and replicable)
- is attuned to and responsive to customer needs (rather than "trying to sell them something they don't really need or want")
- accommodates needs and conflicting demands of its people, using principles of reciprocity
- motivates and engages its people
- cross-pollinates people, ideas, knowledge, points of view

- is transparent and authentic
- is not location-based or location-dependent
- uses sustainable, cradle-to-cradle practices, and does more with less
- engages customers and other partners in design, development and decision-making, to tap into the wisdom of crowds
- has rotating leadership, with leaders who see where the future is going before others do, and inspires others to act on that vision, and who are able to translate the complexity around them into simple truths that have meaning, direction and predictability (rather than encouraging the cult of leadership and the messiah complex of many of today's leaders)
- accommodates and leverages the skills and qualities of women
- finds and clears away obstacles that prevent its people from doing their best
- learns from nature
- teaches people to communicate extraordinarily well, and encourages authentic, powerful conversations
- recognizes our responsibility to leave a legacy for our children, and pays attention to them and learns from them

Sounds good, doesn't it? But suppose half the organizations of the future were like this and the other half were like most of today's traditional large organizations, almost the antithesis of the above. Would customers know, and care, to give their business to the New Age organizations that had these qualities, even if it might cost a bit more to do so? Would employees be willing to forgo higher salaries (and much higher salaries if they reached the top echelons of traditional organizations) for the more human, healthy working environment of the New Age organizations sketched above? Would these New Age organizations work together and prefer dealing with each other rather than dealing with more traditional organizations, and would this preference be enough to counter the oligopoly power that small groups of traditional companies, working in collusion to crush new entrants, wield in many industries?

Part of me is cynical, and thinks this is all wishful thinking. If there had been a few CEOs from large corporations present at the symposium, who could have reassured us (or disillusioned us), that might have been helpful. But part of me is also a believer in models, and I really think that if enough organizations were to emerge that exemplified this New Age behavior, others would follow them, and the traditional model would become intolerable and be discarded, just as the slave-exploiting and robber baron models of industry yielded begrudgingly to better models in the past. What do you think? Is what we envisioned really the organization of the future, or just a dream of incurable optimists?

Model of Good Governance Today
Article is excerpted from a post by Dr. Urmi Ashar
President & CEO of NACD Three Rivers Chapter.
directormuses.wordpress.com

Unfortunately, given the present challenges of the complex world we live in, mere fiduciary oversight is inadequate. Boards must do more than watch the books and stay clear of conflicts of interests. Beyond the duties of care, loyalty, and obedience, there is, I suggest, a fourth board duty: the duty of imagination. It is imperative for boards to imagine the greater potential for the organizations they lead–to envision, create the strategic path, and provide the support for its achievement in the context of greater challenges faced by the society at large. This requires authentic leadership.

While, leadership and management must go hand in hand, they are not the same thing. The manager administers, focuses on execution of systems and relies on control but a leader innovates, focuses on people and inspires trust.

Board leadership will need to build a reputation that will make itself attractive to creative and conceptual thinkers capable of integrative thinking. Integrative thinkers embrace complexity, tolerate uncertainty, and manage tension in searching for creative solutions to problems. Attracting and retaining the right people on your team is the only secret to success and survival in a rapidly changing complex world.

Thus the focus of board leaders will need to be on communicating the right values transparently to earn a reputation of authenticity in the market place! They need to focus on ensuring they have processes and metrics to measure the right culture that fosters the values they want to project in the market place. This will attract and retain creative talent capable of shaping the future. They will need to be proactive in co-operatively working with economic developers to attract the right talent to the region.

If companies care about attracting the right talent and help a region thrive then they must lead the charge for local economic development in the region in partnership with economic developers. It is the highest form of community service and philanthropy. The road map for the economic developers to achieve this will be to thoroughly scan the environment of the region and ensure there are adequate avenues available in the fabric of the region comprised of the start-up ventures, non-profits and public-private partnerships to encourage the emergence of such talent and the maturation of their leadership. In short the leadership of economic development in this regard cannot be underestimated. The corporate and economic development leadership will need to partner in zealously creating regional systems that are attractive to creative and conceptual thinkers capable of integrative thinking. Integrative thinkers embrace complexity, tolerate uncertainty, and manage tension in searching for creative solutions to problems. They are not simply efficient drones diligent in execution.

The current leadership on corporate and non-profit boards along with the economic development leadership will need to interpret the market demands of today and must create a willingness in their own constituencies to move beyond resisting and "dealing with" change. This is now not simply an ideal on the wish list but a first order need for survival in order to tap the opportunity inherent in connecting with the key constituents in the marketplace.

The most successful organizations and regions will have to focus on attracting and enabling those that are able to invent the future, and are not only able to leverage the strengths and but are also able to effectively manage the weaknesses to realize success. The mindset has to be that of constant awareness and ability to embrace ambiguity and to learn, unlearn and relearn on the fly. The emphasis has to be in creating conditions conducive for survival of intrinsically motivated people whose drivers are: autonomy, mastery, and a sense of purpose.

In order to manage reputation effectively leadership will also have to focus on ability to innovate. Intangible assets will provide private sector in gaining the competitive edge in the fourth economy, which is firmly rooted in technology, supported by innovation and knowledge networks. In order to become sustainable businesses will focus on their own value propositions such that they can adapt to the world's changing needs and the dynamic seismic shifts in the market place.

Real leadership is less about handwringing and lamenting about an era gone by but more about confronting the realities and constraints of shrinking resources and unleashing the potential of the people it attracts to create an economically vibrant tapestry. This brand of leadership has to emerge simultaneously in the private as well as public sector Today board leadership stretches beyond fiduciary responsibilities to effective management of reputation. It is that fourth duty: *The Duty of Imagination*, which will attract and empower those that are capable of shaping the future.

The Benjamin Franklin Method for Managing by Virtues
By C. Dan McArthur and Larry G. Womack

Preface

Contrary to what you may have heard, virtues continue to drive most business decisions. In our years of management consulting we've never worked with a mentally healthy manager who didn't want to do the right thing.

There have, of course, been situations where unwise decisions were made, but even in those cases the motivation was usually to do what was thought best. We all from time to time act purely in our own self-interest. From our consulting experiences, though, we have learned that most actions in business settings are reactions to the organization's culture – not selfishly motivated.

People usually do whatever is expected of them. If the environment encourages protectionism and tail-covering, that will be the order of the day. If leadership sets a tone of cooperation and a spirit of "all for one and one for all" the atmosphere will be collegial.

Webster defines virtue as conformity to a standard of right. Benjamin Franklin established his own standards of right and tried to live by them. The purpose of this article is to assist you to establish your standards of right and to provide you a methodology for living to those standards. Benjamin Franklin's method serves as the basis of our methodology. You must create your own standard.

We've taken Ben Franklin's definition of each virtue and updated it in contemporary language. Our definitions are there as guidelines for you to create your standards of right.

Ben Franklin
"A penny saved is a penny earned."

Benjamin Franklin (1706 – 1790) was a jack-of-all trades and master of many. No other American, except possibly Thomas Jefferson, has done so many things well. During his long and useful life, Franklin concerned himself with such different matters as statesmanship and soap making, book printing and cabbage growing, and the rise of tides and the fall of empires. He invented an efficient heading stove and proved that lightning is electricity.

As a statesman, Franklin stood in the front rank of the men who build the United States of America. He was the only man who signed all four key documents in American history – the Declaration of Independence, the Treaty of Alliance with France, the Treaty of Peace with Great Britain, and the Constitutions of the United States. Franklin's services as minister to France were instrumental in winning the Revolutionary War. Many historians consider him the ablest and most successful diplomat American has ever sent abroad.

Franklin was a major contributor of his day to the study of electricity. As an inventor he was unequaled in the United States until the time of Thomas Edison. People still quote from Franklin's *Saying of Poor Richard* and read his *Autobiography*. Franklin founded Pennsylvania's first university and its first public hospital.

Franklin's fame also extended to Europe. In this country, Thomas Jefferson hailed him as "the greatest man and ornament of the age and of the country in which he lived." A French Statesman, Count Honore de Mirabeau, called him "the sage whom two worlds claimed as their own."

It has also been said that Franklin was America's first economist. He wrote numerous papers on money, national wealth, credit, wages, the movement of populations, and other economic subjects.

Much of the material in *Poor Richard's Almanac* was devoted to economic issues, as were his many contributions to the European press. His views on economics were similar to many of the mid twentieth-century economists. Franklin believed that economics was the handmaiden of political expediency.

Managing by Virtue
"To err is human, to repent divine; to persist devilish"

While pursuing his business opportunities, Franklin always found time for continual soul searching and examination of his own code of virtue. In his *Autobiography* he describes how he undertook to continually improve himself morally and ethically.

It was about this time I conceived the bold and arduous project of arriving at moral perfection. I wished to live without committing any fault at any time; I would conquer all either natural inclination, custom, or company might lead me into.

As I knew, or thought I knew, what was right and wrong, I did not see why I might not always do the one and avoid the other. But I soon found I had undertaken a task of more difficulty than I had imagined. While my care was employed in guarding against one fault, I was often surprised by another; habit took the advantage of inattention; inclination was sometimes too strong for reason.

I concluded, at length, that the mere speculative conviction that it was our interest to be completely virtuous was not sufficient to prevent our slipping; and that the contrary habits must be broken, and good ones acquired and established, before we can have any dependence upon a steady, uniform rectitude of conduct. For this purpose I therefore contrived the following method.

In the various enumerations of moral virtues I had met with in my reading, I found the catalog more or less numerous, as different writers included more or fewer ideas under the same name.

Temperance, for example, was by some confined to eating and drinking, while by others it was extended to mean the moderating of every other pleasure, appetite, inclination, or passion, bodily or mental, even to avarice and ambition.

I proposed to myself, for the sake of clearness, to use rather more names, with fewer ideas annexed to each, than few names with more ideas; and I included, under thirteen names of virtues, all that at time occurred to me as necessary or desirable, and annexed to each a short precept, which fully expressed the extent I gave to its meaning.

These names of virtue, with their precepts, were:

1. *Temperance - eat not to dullness; drink not to elation.*
2. *Silence - Speak not but what may benefit others or yourself; avoid trifling conversation.*
3. *Order - Let all your things have their places; let each part of your business have its time.*
4. *Resolution - Resolve to perform what you ought; perform without fail what you resolve.*
5. *Frugality - Make no expense but to do good to others or yourself; that is, waste nothing.*
6. *Industry - Lose no time; be always employed in something useful; cut off all unnecessary actions.*
7. *Sincerity - Use no hurtful deceit; think innocently and justly; speak accordingly.*
8. *Justice - Wrong none by doing injuries; or omitting the benefits of your duty.*
9. *Moderation - Avoid extremes; forbear resenting injuries so much as you think they deserve.*
10. *Cleanliness - Tolerate no uncleanliness in body, clothes, or habitation.*
11. *Tranquility - Be not disturbed at trifles or at accidents common or unavoidable.*
12. *Chastity - Rarely use venery but for health or offspring, never to dullness, weakness, or the injury of your own or another's peace or reputation*
13. *Humility – Imitate Jesus and Socrates*

Franklin determined that it would be impossible to acquire the "complete habitude" of all the virtues all at one time. He decided to master them in the order of their acquisition as they are presented. Franklin put Temperance first.

Temperance tends to procure that coolness and clearness of head, which is so necessary where constant vigilance was to be kept up, and guard maintained against the unremitting attraction of ancient habits, and the force of perpetual temptations. This being acquired and established, Silence would be more easy.

Benjamin Franklin made a book in which he allotted a page for each virtue. He ruled the pages with red ink, so as to have seven columns, one for each day of the week, and marked each column with a letter for the day. He then drew thirteen horizontal lines and marked the beginning of each with the first letter of the virtue it represented. With every fault he found upon reflection of his daily activities he placed a black dot in the appropriate square.

I determined to give a week's strict attention to each of the virtues successively. Thus, in the first week, my greatest guard was to avoid even the least offense against Temperance, leaving the other virtues in their ordinary chance, only marking every evening the faults of the day. Thus, if in the first week I could keep my first line, marked T, clear of spots, I supposed the habit of that virtue so much strengthened, and its opposite weakened, that I might venture extending my attention to include the next, and for the following week keep both lines clear of spots.

In truth, I found myself incorrigible with respect to Order; and now I am grown old, and my memory bad, I feel very sensibly the want of it. But, on the whole, though I never arrived at the perfection I had been so ambitious of obtaining, but fell far short of it, yet I was, by the endeavor, a better and a happier man than I otherwise should have been if I had not attempted it.

Temperance: Eat not to dullness. Drink not to elevation							
	S	M	T	W	T	F	S
T – Temperance							
S – Silence	..	.		.		.	
O – Order	.	.	.		.	.	.
R - Resolution			.			.	
F - Frugality		.			.		
I – Industry			.				
S – Sincerity							
J – Justice							
M – Moderation							
CL – Cleanliness							
T – Tranquility							
Ch – Chastity							
H - Humility							

Those who aim at perfect writing by imitating the engraved copies, though they never reach the wished for excellence of those copies, their hand is mended by the endeavor.

Benjamin Franklin's quest for perfection provided him a process for achieving a higher level of performance in his work, greater satisfaction from his relationships with others, and a method for ensuring that each aspect of his life received appropriate and timely attention. Benjamin Franklin managed his affairs by virtues and achieved a degree of greatness and recognition few have ever known.

As you review the thirteen virtues of Franklin that we have modernized to address today's complexities of business, develop your own set of virtues that you would like to master. Think about the individuals whom you admire most. What characteristics do they possess that you would most like to emulate?

One

TEMPERANCE

Eat not to dullness; drink not to elevation

Be consistent in thought, action, and feeling

As a manager, it is your job to empower others to strive for excellence in their work. People work hard for managers who are fair, visible, reachable, consistent, and who practice what they preach. Excessive control, inspection, and instruction are a waste of everyone's time. Managers must manage outcomes and allow their charges to manage themselves. Be firm, open, consistent and temperate in all that you do and everyone will be better for it, including you.

"This easier to suppress the first desire than to satisfy all that follow it. "

Two

SILENCE

Speak not but what may benefit others or yourself;
Avoid trifling conversation

Communication requires a sender and a receiver.
Be a receiver most of the time.

Managing is more listening than talking.   Because people learn as much when they talk as when they listen, allow your people to talk to you without fear or concern for consequences. Encourage your people to listen to heir co-workers and subordinates. The best ideas often flow upstream.

"A good example is the best sermon"

Three

ORDER

Let all your things have their places;
Let each part of your business have its time

Dream before you think, think before you plan,
and plan before you act

It is impossible to achieve a desired outcome without a plan.
Your role as a manager is to plan outcomes and empower your
people to achieve them. If you cannot tell your people where you
want to go, how can they help you get there? Begin your
planning by first dreaming, then thinking, then planning. You'll
find the challenge greater and the results more rewarding.

"He that by the plow would thrive,
himself must either hold or drive"

Four

RESOLUTION

Resolve to perform what you ought;
perform without fail what you resolve

Do as I say. Do as I do.

Managing people at labor is no different than leading a family. It is important to clearly articulate the requirements of membership. It is also important to set the example of leadership by following through. Collaboration does not mean democratizing the decision-making process. It does mean, however, tapping all the sources of knowledge that are available and developing a consensus from the collected wisdom. Followers respect firm leaders, if they are right in their firmness.

"He that cannot obey cannot command"

Five

FRUGALITY

Make no expense but to do good yourself;
ie, waste nothing

Improving quality and productivity,
And cost will go down

The manager's job is not to control cost. It is to elevate performance. The manager should concentrate on helping people work smarter. The end result is always cost savings. Teach your people how to do their job right the first time, and the cost of doing business will automatically decrease.

"An ounce of prevention is worth a pound of cure"

Six

INDUSTRY

*Lose no time; be always employed in something useful;
cut off all unnecessary actions*

If it doesn't add value don't do it!

A manager must continuously review the work to ensure that form always follows function. By focusing on the outcome instead of the tasks, it is often possible to eliminate steps in the process. People enjoy useful labor. Be sure your people enjoy their work. If they do, they will choose to do more of it.

"The noblest question in the world is,
'What good may I do in it?'"

Seven

SINCERITY

Use no hurtful deceit; think innocently and justly,
and if you speak, speak accordingly

If you speak the truth you will hear the truth

Whenever there is fear in an organization, people tell management what they think management wants to hear. Fear almost always arises from misinformation. It is the responsibility of a manager to provide an atmosphere of trust. If your people trust you they will tell you what you need to hear, not what they think you want to hear.

"To err is human, to repent divine; to persist devilish"

Eight

JUSTICE

Wrong none by doing injuries,
or omitting the benefits that are your duty

If there is wrong, right it. If there is a right, praise it.

With the responsibility of management comes authority. It is your job to recognize the frailties of the system. Sometimes that means reprimanding unacceptable behavior. Be swift, clear, and appropriate in your actions. Your people will respect your forthrightness and appreciate your willingness to assume the burden of leadership.

"He that lieth down with dogs shall rise with fleas"

Nine

MODERATION

Avoid extremes; forbear resenting injuries
so much as you think they deserve

Be even handed, even tempered, and even fun!

Present a consistent view of your expectations, your respect for tasks, and for the individuals who perform the task. The role of the manager is to empower through example. The best example is consistency and an even approach to people.

"There's a time to wink as well as a to see"

Ten

CLEANLINESS

Tolerate no uncleanliness in body, clothing, or habitation

Respect the space, the possessions, and the rights of others

Most people spend the majority of their waking hours at work. Encourage respect for the workplace by being respectful of it. The violation of one's privacy at home or at the office is unconscionable. Commons areas belong to everyone, not the company. If the manager is respectful of privacy, responsible for order, and respectful of the environment, compliance from everyone is implied and need not be required.

"When you are good to others, you are best to yourself"

Eleven

TRANQUILITY

Be not disturbed at trifles,
or at accidents common or unavoidable

Most mistakes are caused by the process, not by the people

A good manager looks at what is better, not at who is wrong.
Solutions come from examining the process, not from assessing
blame. Learn to take work, but not yourself, seriously.
Recognize that people almost always want to do their best. Don't
be disturbed by failure. Use it as a lesson learned and a block on
which to build a better process.

"Write injuries in dust, benefits in marble"

Twelve

CHASTITY

Rarely use venery but for health or offspring, never to dullness, weakness, or the injury of your own or another's peace or reputation

Celebrate the diversity of humanity and respect its intentions

The manager is the arbiter of justice in the workplace. Derogatory remarks and disrespect for persons of difference must not be tolerated. The manager must set the example of respect with swift corrective action when harm has occurred. And must do so in practice and belief, and sometimes with a sense of humor.

"All blood is alike ancient"

Thirteen

HUMILITY

Imitate Jesus and Socrates

Love your neighbor and feed your brain

The successful manager is one who recognizes that personal growth comes from gaining new knowledge and empowering others through the knowledge gained. There is no greater reward than to provide the wisdom for another to succeed. The best managers are those who encourage learning by example and providing regular educational opportunities for those they lead.

"Content makes poor men rich;
discontent makes rich men poor"

Managing buy Virtue Exercise

Benjamin Franklin developed a very detailed method for improving the way he managed his life, conducted his business, and related to others. His method and his definition of virtue served as a thoughtful background from which to develop a personal program of self-improvement. We discovered Franklin's method during the development of a leadership workshop for our clients. Our goal was to help the attendees create an ongoing process of improvement, rather than to just raise the awareness to the value of continuously evaluating one's ability.

Often the important lessons learned in workshops and seminars fade with time, if a simple process isn't provided to keep the lesson alive and meaningful. What follows is the experience from our leadership workshops. Once you have mastered the concept, we recommend that you share the process with your friends, family and co-workers

Managing by Virtue

Who are the people you admire most and what are the reasons for your admiration? Think of three individuals living or dead and write your choices on the form below or on a blank sheet of paper. If you wish to share the experience with others, do not write in the book. The persons whom you admire may be friends, co-workers, or from business, religion, sports, entertainment, politics, or any walk of life. List them below and identify three characteristics that set these persons apart from the ordinary.

Person #1:
Characteristics:
A.

B.

C.

Person #2:
Characteristics:
A.

B.

C.

Person #3:
Characteristics:
A.

B.

C.

Using a scale of 1 to 5 (5 being excellent), rate yourself against the characteristics of those whom you admire. Write the number beside the characteristic.

Make a list below of the virtues by which you would like to manage your business and personal affairs. Select your virtues from your list, Franklin's list, and any other source you can find. You need not be as ambitious as Ben Franklin. Select as many as you think you can reasonably manage.

1.

2.

3.

4.

5.

6.

7.

8.

9.

10.

11.

12.

13.

INSTRUCTIONS

1. Make the same number of copies of this blank chart as the number of virtues you have identified for yourself.
2. Write a virtue at the top of each page
3. Organize the pages in the order you want to address them.
4. Identify the virtues alongside the appropriate order. Franklin just used the first letter.
5. Beginning on the next Sunday, start managing your life to the first virtue you select.

	S	M	T	W	T	F	S

Franklin's words about his virtue process deserves repeating.

I determined to give a week's strict attention to each of the virtues successively. Thus, in the first week, my greatest guard was to avoid even the least offense against Temperance, leaving the other virtues in their ordinary chance, only marking every evening the faults of the day. Thus, if in the first week I could keep my first line, marked T, clear of spots, I supposed the habit of that virtue so much strengthened, and its opposite weakened, that I might venture extending my attention to include the next, and for the following week keep both lines clear of spots.

In truth, I found myself incorrigible with respect to Order; and now I am grown old, and my memory bad, I feel very sensibly the want of it. But, on the whole, though I never arrived at the perfection I had been so ambitious of obtaining, but fell far short of it, yet I was, by the endeavor, a better and a happier man than I otherwise should have been if I had not attempted it.

Those who aim at perfect writing by imitating the engraved copies, though they never reach the wished for excellence of those copies, their hand is mended by the endeavor.

The Authors

Dan McArthur is an independent board director and a member of the *Institute for Effective Leadership advisory board.* He has been a top-tier management consulting firm leadership principal, senior manager in several major corporations, managing director of a private equity firm and an entrepreneur. He is author of *Outcome Management* and many other books and articles on business vitality.

Vincent Higgins is a board director, strategist and President and CEO of the *Institute for Effective Leadership.* With advanced degrees in physics, philosophy, and theology, he uses his "theophysicist" background in *leadership and enterprise development.* He has lived in a number of countries working with corporate leaders and organizations and speaks several languages.

The Institute for Effective Leadership, a leadership development and advisory firm which sees "effectiveness" as achieving --and constantly surpassing-- an organization's stated objectives, for greater impact, profitability and sustainability. Its proven track record has enabled executives and decision-makers to reach their full potential, for the good of their organizations and society as a whole. www.effective-leadership.com.

Endorsements

"Einstein said that everything should be made as simple as possible ... but no simpler. McArthur and Higgins have managed to accomplish that delicate balance in the field of leadership ... they have simplified the academic research so that it has practical utility while avoiding the oversimplification trap into which other practical leadership books fall"

Bruce Hamilton
CEO, Energy Company &
U.S. Navy Captain (retired)

"*Social Influence and Genius* provides the big picture and detailed character traits to be an effective leader and is full of examples, questions and other tools to help raise the leadership and cultural corpus of an individual or organization. The chapters on Culture, Alignment and Imperative's are a must for the Chief Operating and Corporate Compliance Officers. The book is an eclectic tome on leadership for the novice or most experienced professional"

Daniel Torpey, CPA, CFF, CITP
Partner, Ernst & Young, LLP

"If I had read *Social Influence and Genius* 20 years ago, I would have been and the businesses I managed would have been much more successful. The book will rapidly become a best seller. I truly could not put it down!"

Joseph Nassif, Area Manager, Nustar Energy Corporation
Fortune Magazine's top 100 best companies to work for in 2011.

"*Social Influence and Genius* clearly brings to light the elements of a true leader, showing how personal and financial success are built. The authors deftly expose the true meaning of leadership, a life-long journey that provides tangible results, both in profits and in deeper meaning."

Carlos E. Gonzalez, Managing Director
Northgulf Partners Inc (Financial Services)

"Higgins and McArthur have unveiled the essence of true leadership with their introduction of the "Leadership Trilogy" and the unlocking of an organization's "Genius Network"! The pyramid symbolism throughout their writings provide a level of simplicity that is easily understood by both junior and senior leadership today. It provides an in depth comprehension of skills and attributes needed to lead in the 21st century. A fresh and sophisticated new look at Leadership. I will recommend and provide this masterpiece to all my corporate clients."

Jim Bethmann, Managing Partner
Caldwell Partners (Executive Search)

Index

www.ingramcontent.com/pod-product-compliance
Lightning Source LLC
Chambersburg PA
CBHW070534200326
41519CB00013B/3041